God ❤ Me

3-MINUTE DEVOTIONS

for Girls on the Go!

Published by Barbour Books, an imprint of Barbour Publishing, Inc., P.O. Box 719, Uhrichsville, Ohio 44683, www.barbourbooks.com

Our mission is to publish and distribute inspirational products offering exceptional value and biblical encouragement to the masses.

Member of the
Evangelical Christian
Publishers Association

Printed in the United States of America.

05015 0315 DP

God ♥s me

3-MINUTE DEVOTIONS

for Girls on the Go!

MariLee Parrish

BARBOUR BOOKS
An Imprint of Barbour Publishing, Inc.

Introduction

My theme song is God's love.

PSALM 101:1 MSG

Take a few moments of your day to quiet your spirit, think on God's amazing love for you, and make a meaningful connection with your heavenly Father.

Minute 1: Meditate on a brief scripture selection.

Minute 2: Read through the devotional.

Minute 3: Read the prayer to help jump-start a conversation with God.

Just 3 short minutes, and you'll be blessed with beautiful inspiration and encouragement for your young heart!

What Will You Choose?

*But the Holy Spirit produces this kind of fruit
in our lives: love, joy, peace, patience, kindness,
goodness, faithfulness, gentleness, and self-control.
There is no law against these things!*

GALATIANS 5:22–23 NLT

When you first choose to follow Christ, the Spirit of God
Himself comes to live inside of you (see Romans 8:9)! How
amazing is that? God loves you so much that He could
never leave you alone down here. He actually sent His
Spirit to live right inside of you to help you and guide you
in this mixed-up world. If you truly belong to Jesus, He
starts changing you from the inside out! He replaces the
old you—the one that struggled with anger and selfish-
ness—and starts filling you with love. . .joy. . .peace. . .
patience, and kindness. Wait. . .there's more! The Spirit will
also teach you how to choose goodness, to be faithful and
gentle, and to have self-control! We don't have to figure
any of that stuff out on our own.

Here's the thing: if you haven't chosen to follow Christ,
you'll always be missing that supernatural power that God
places inside your heart when you come to know Him.
Take a minute right now and decide how you want to live.
Do you want to live with the power of Christ—or without it?
Nobody can make that choice but you.

*God, I choose to trust You with my life. I want the power
that You offer to change me from the inside out. I know
You love me. Will You teach me how to love You back?*

I'm Your Friend

*I have called you friends, for everything that I learned
from my Father I have made known to you. You did not
choose me, but I chose you and appointed you so that
you might go and bear fruit—fruit that will last—and so
that whatever you ask in my name the Father will
give you. This is my command: Love each other.*

JOHN 15:15–17 NIV

God wants to be your friend.

What?!

Yep, God wants to be your friend!

Whatever you may have heard about God from other
people—including the idea that God is just a big grumpy
grandpa sitting at the edge of heaven looking down to see
if you're being good or bad—if it doesn't line up with what
the Bible says about God, it's simply not true. The truth is
that God wants to be your friend. Jesus said so Himself.
Jesus showed up on our planet to show us His love and to
teach us to love each other. He's all about having a relationship—a friendship—with you!

*God, thanks for wanting my friendship. Help me
to jump into Your Word and find out the truth
about who You are and how much You love me.*

A Love That Is Faithful

Give thanks to the LORD, for he is good!
His faithful love endures forever.
PSALM 107:1 NLT

There is no one else on this earth who can be faithful to
you all the time. Not your parents, not your best friend, not
people you trust from church. . .no one gets it right all the
time. No one, that is, except Jesus. Jesus directs all His
love and faithfulness right toward you. He will never leave
you. He'll never give up on you. He'll never lie to you. He'll
never ever stop loving you. Nothing you could ever do
will ever change His mind about how much He loves you.
That's a big deal! The biggest! God looks at you and smiles
because He sees Jesus in you. God is your loving parent
who never gets it wrong. You don't have to be afraid to talk
to Him or tell Him what's going on in your life. He already
knows, and He wants to hear from you anyway.

God, I want to know more about You, and I
want to grow closer to You each day. Thank You
for Your amazing love and faithfulness to me.

Your Love Is My Song

*Your love, GOD, is my song, and I'll sing it! I'm forever
telling everyone how faithful you are. I'll never
quit telling the story of your love—how you built
the cosmos and guaranteed everything in it.*

PSALM 89:1-2 MSG

. . . .

God shows His love for us in many, many ways. One of the
simplest ways to actually see God's love is to go outside
and experience His works for yourself. You can see His
handiwork in the flowers and trees in spring and summer.
The bright leaves changing in the fall and the blankets of
snow He sends in the winter. The skies tell of His wonders
in every season. Animals and creatures great and small
know their Creator. The birds that God created are always
singing His praises as they go about their busy tasks. . .and
you can, too. God gave you your voice to talk to Him, to tell
of His great love, and to sing His praises every day of your
life.

*I love to sing, God, even though I may not be that
good at it. Thank You that Your love can and will be
my song. . .forever! Help me never to quit telling the
story of Your love. . .or singing about it.*

That Faithful Love, Again

Praise GOD, everybody! Applaud GOD, all people!
His love has taken over our lives; GOD's faithful
ways are eternal. Hallelujah!

PSALM 117:1–2 MSG

. . . .

All throughout the book of Psalms in the Bible you will
hear verses like the one above. Here are a few more:

Give thanks to the LORD, for he is good!
His faithful love endures forever.

PSALM 136:1 NLT

Give thanks to him who alone does mighty miracles.
His faithful love endures forever.

PSALM 136:4 NLT

You'll find evidence of God's faithful love all throughout the Bible. In fact, that's really what it's all about. Don't
ever forget it. God's love is faithful and enduring even
when everyone else's love fades away. Jesus is the one you
can turn to at all times. He wants to celebrate with you in
good times and comfort you in bad times. When everyone
else is on your case, He will lovingly stand beside you
and lead you into His truth and grace. You'll never have a
better friend than Jesus.

Thank You again and again for Your great love for me,
Jesus. I believe that You are faithful and that You'll
always love me and be with me, no matter what.

And Again!

The LORD will work out his plans for my life—
for your faithful love, O LORD, endures forever.
Don't abandon me, for you made me.

PSALM 138:8 NLT

Again, God's love for you is unfailing and faithful. He is with you always. He is listening, and He loves you like you're the only girl in the universe! You are His princess, and He will never abandon you. You are a daughter of the King of all kings, and He has wonderful plans for your life. Even the painful things that happen in life, God will miraculously turn into good things if you trust in Him! Check out Romans 8:28 (NIV), which says, "And we know that in all things God works for the good of those who love him, who have been called according to his purpose." Pretty amazing, huh? As you grow up, you're going to have a lot of distractions in life, trying to get you to turn away from trusting in God's great love for you. That's our enemy's one purpose in this life. So, remember how much God loves you and hide this verse in your heart. Memorize it, and allow the Holy Spirit to bring it to your mind anytime you start to forget.

God, I pray that You would keep me from getting
too distracted in this life. I want to follow You.

God Knows Me

You have searched me, LORD, and you know me.
You know when I sit and when I rise; you perceive my
thoughts from afar. You discern my going out and my
lying down; you are familiar with all my ways. Before a
word is on my tongue you, LORD, know it completely.

PSALM 139:1–4 NIV

Did you know that God actually knows *you*? Not just your
family or the pastor at whatever church you may have
attended—but He knows *you*! Personally. Intimately. The
Bible tells us He knows how many hairs are on our heads.
Before we say a word, He knows what it will be. He knows
when you're going to sit down, stand up, go shopping,
think a thought—everything! Even if you've ignored God
every day before now, He hasn't ignored you. Open your
Bible and read the rest of Psalm 139. Even though there
are billions of people in this world, God made you and He
cares about you. He knows your name. He loves you more
than you could ever imagine.

God, will You open up my heart so that I can be fully
aware of You? I want to see You at work in my life.

The Perfect Parent

So the LORD must wait for you to come to him
so he can show you his love and compassion.
For the LORD is a faithful God. Blessed are those
who wait for his help.

ISAIAH 30:18 NLT

. . . .

Have you ever longed for something? It's where you want something so bad and can hardly wait until it happens. Another version of this verse (NIV) says "the LORD longs to be gracious to you." God does not force Himself on anyone. That was never His plan. He has made it clear who He is and what He's done. . .and then He waits for us to come to Him. His desire is to shower you with love and compassion, but He won't do it unless you let Him. And He longs for you to let Him bless You. Everything that happens to you in this life is for your good and God's glory. Imagine a parent who loves you unconditionally and never, ever makes a mistake. That's who God is. He meets all your needs and will give you the desires of your heart when you follow Him.

Thank You for being my perfect parent, Father.
I choose to come to You each day, trusting You
want the very best for me.

Our First Love

*For God so loved the world that he gave his one
and only Son, that whoever believes in him
shall not perish but have eternal life.*

JOHN 3:16 NIV

. . . .

The ancient philosopher St. Augustine said that "God loves each of us as if there were only one of us." Do you personally believe that is true? First John 4:9–10 (NIV) says: "This is how God showed his love among us: He sent his one and only Son into the world that we might live through him. This is love: not that we loved God, but that he loved us and sent his Son as an atoning sacrifice for our sins." Sometimes it's hard to know how to love God back after such a sacrifice. When we follow God's Word, listen for His voice, and love others. . .that is how we show love to God. And when we aren't sure what to do or how to love? "We know and rely on the love God has for us" (1 John 4:16 NIV).

*God, Your love for me is overwhelming sometimes. In a good
way! But I don't know how I can love You back like that.
So, please help me to listen for Your voice in my life and to
follow after You, relying on the love You have for me.*

A Life of Love

God is love. When we take up permanent residence in a life of love, we live in God and God lives in us.
1 JOHN 4:17 MSG

. . . .

Did you know that the biblical definition of love is God? God = love. Love = God. This world has a really messed up view of love. Most people think love is a feeling of happiness, but that's not always true. Love is a choice. You can still choose to love someone even if you don't feel like it. First Corinthians 13:4–8 (NIV) tells us a little bit more of what true love is like: "Love is patient, love is kind. It does not envy, it does not boast, it is not proud. It does not dishonor others, it is not self-seeking, it is not easily angered, it keeps no record of wrongs. Love does not delight in evil but rejoices with the truth. It always protects, always trusts, always hopes, always perseveres. Love never fails." That's a lot different than the way Hollywood paints it, right? When you choose a life of love, it won't always be easy. It means you're always seeking God's will instead of your own. God will bless you abundantly for it!

God, please help me to choose love instead of my own way.

The Truth about Love

My dear friends, don't believe everything you hear.
Carefully weigh and examine what people tell you.
Not everyone who talks about God comes from God.

1 JOHN 4:1 MSG

Our enemy likes to trick people. He's really good at it. He likes to deceive, and the Bible says that he even disguises himself as an angel of light (see 2 Corinthians 11:14)! So ask God to give you wisdom about this. There are a lot of people in this world that like to talk about God. They use God's Word to serve their own purposes, but their hearts are far from Him. Always test what people say about God with His Word. Look it up and research the context of the Bible. People like to take certain verses out of the Bible and use them to say what they want it to say. Find a study Bible or an online study Bible and find out what God's Word really says. You have the Spirit of God right there in your heart, so if someone says something about God and it doesn't quite feel right, check it out.

God, please give me wisdom about You.
Thank You that I have Your Spirit to guide me.

God's Voice Vs. Satan's Voice

Do you presume on the riches of his kindness and forbearance and patience, not knowing that God's kindness is meant to lead you to repentance?
ROMANS 2:4 ESV

There is a picture of someone's journal that has gone around Facebook. It lists the characteristics of God's voice versus the characteristics of our enemy. It notes that God's voice stills, leads, reassures, enlightens, comforts, calms and convicts while our enemy's voice rushes, pushes, frightens, confuses, discourages, worries, obsesses, and condemns. Which voice are you listening to?

People often take on the characteristics of our enemy, too, often without even knowing it. Beware of friends or family members who frighten, confuse, and condemn you. That is not loving, and it is not from God. When God convicts you of sin, He does so with kindness that leads you back to Him. He never shames or condemns you (see John 3:17).

God, thank You for Your loving voice that calls me back to the protection of Your arms. Help me to be wise in the relationships I form. Help me to find good and loving relationships that encourage my faith and trust in You.

What Does God Think of You?

So God created human beings in his image. In the image of God he created them. He created them male and female.
GENESIS 1:27 NCV

. . . .

Not only is God the creator of the Universe, He created *you*! In His image. While He was forming your heart, the Bible tells us that He set eternity right there inside (see Ecclesiastes 3:11). So as long as we live, we will never be made whole until we have made peace with our Creator— until we've accepted His love and begin to live out a daily relationship with Him.

You never have to wonder what God thinks about you. He tells you plainly how much He loves and cares for you. God's Word says this:

You are free and clean in the blood of Christ.

- He has rescued you from darkness and has brought you into His kingdom.
- You are a precious child of the Father.
- God sings over you.
- He delights in you.
- You are a friend of Christ.
- Nothing can separate you from God's love.
- God knows you intimately.
- God sees you as beautiful, and you are wonderfully made.
- God is for you, not against you!

Wow! Thank You, God. . . Thank You!

Heart and Soul

*Everyone who confesses that Jesus is God's Son
participates continuously in an intimate relationship
with God. We know it so well, we've embraced it heart
and soul, this love that comes from God.*

1 JOHN 4:15–16 MSG

John wrote this letter to early Christians who had gotten
off track. They were conforming more and more to what
the world wanted them to do and be—instead of what God
wanted them to do and be. Sounds familiar right? That's
why God's Word is living and active and still very much
applies to us today. John and the other followers of Jesus
had developed an intimate relationship with God through
Jesus. John reminds us that this relationship is possible
for all of us. God wants us to know Him personally! We can
embrace Christ with all of our hearts. Well, what does that
look like today? It's listening for God and getting to know
His voice. That gentle voice that encourages and comforts
us. Ask God to make Himself known to you and He will. . .if
you're listening.

*God, please help me get to know Your voice. I want to love
You with all of my heart and soul. Lead me as I grow up
knowing and following You.*

Joy in Your Presence

You make known to me the path of life;
you will fill me with joy in your presence,
with eternal pleasures at your right hand.

PSALM 16:11 NIV

God promises to fill us with His joy—and we don't have to wait until heaven for that! We have access to His peace, joy, grace, and presence right now while we live on earth through the power of the Holy Spirit. Hebrews 4:15–16 says: "We don't have a priest who is out of touch with our reality. He's been through weakness and testing, experienced it all—all but the sin. So let's walk right up to him and get what he is so ready to give." How cool is that? Just walk right up to him and He will fill you with peace and joy in His presence. God is with you in this very moment. If you're having trouble feeling joy in your life, get alone somewhere and just talk to God. Tell God exactly how you feel—either out loud, in your mind, or jot it in a journal.

God, I ask that You would fill me with joy in Your presence.
I want Your constant presence in my life
and the joy that only You can give.

Can I Really Have Joy When Life Hurts?

Dear friends, do not be surprised at the fiery ordeal that has come on you to test you, as though something strange were happening to you. But rejoice inasmuch as you participate in the sufferings of Christ, so that you may be overjoyed when his glory is revealed.

1 PETER 4:12–13 NIV

Life in a messed-up world can be difficult. Jesus himself told us we're going to have trouble here, so we should expect it. Yet he also said, "Take heart! I have overcome the world" (John 16:33). How can we live with joy in our hearts while we're expecting trouble? Well, we wake up each morning expecting some challenges and we ask God to help us through each and every one. We don't have to be negative all the time, expecting the worst. Always look at trouble as a challenge that can be overcome with the power of Christ. When trouble comes, we are sharing in the sufferings of Christ—and that is a powerful thing. We can find Christ in each trial, and He will give us joy in His presence!

Jesus, I'm expecting some challenges today, and I know You will be with me through them all. Please give me Your power and wisdom to get through each one.

Life Can Be Tough

*Now if we are children, then we are heirs—heirs of God
and co-heirs with Christ, if indeed we share in his
sufferings in order that we may also share in his glory.*

ROMANS 8:17 NIV

. . . .

A broken heart, a friend who lets you down, a problem at
school, someone you love dies or moves away. . .life can
be tough. When we go through times of great pain and
difficulty in our lives, we have the opportunity to get closer
to Christ and share the suffering or push God away and
become bitter. Have you ever seen a beautiful bitter person? Probably not. When we allow bitterness to consume
us, it can start to turn us ugly from the inside out. Yet
when we share our sufferings with Christ and allow Him
to fill us with His peace and presence, His light shines in
the darkest places. . .filling us with His kind of beauty. So
when life is tough, ask Jesus to fill you up. He will provide
everything you need to live this life with joy.

*Jesus, shine Your light into the dark places in my life.
I want to be filled with Your light and love.*

Life Can Be Wonderful

*May the God of hope fill you with all joy and peace
as you trust in him, so that you may overflow with hope
by the power of the Holy Spirit.*

ROMANS 15:13 NIV

Think of a person you know who loves God with her whole heart and seeks to follow Him in everything she does. Is there a special light in her eyes and an unshakeable hope in her heart? God can fill you with that very same kind of hope and joy. When you commit to follow Christ, the God of all hope changes you. In good times and bad, you can still overflow with hope because of the power of the Holy Spirit living inside of You. This makes life wonderful and worth living. . .even during difficult times. Pray to the God of hope, and ask Him to fill you to overflowing. He will do it!

*God of Hope, thank You for giving me life. Light up my eyes
and my soul with Your joy and peace. Let others see the
difference in me so that I can point them to You.*

An Attitude of Joy

May the God who gives endurance and encouragement give you the same attitude of mind toward each other that Christ Jesus had, so that with one mind and one voice you may glorify the God and Father of our Lord Jesus Christ.

ROMANS 15:5-6 NIV

You have a choice every day when you wake up. You can choose to be thankful for a new day and look at it with joy and hopeful expectation, or you can choose to let the day get ahead of you and spend the rest of the day trying to catch up. The second choice happens a lot if we aren't careful; and instead of looking at each moment as a gift, we are full of stress and worry. Ask God to help you see each new day as a gift. As you wake up, ask Him to go before you and remind you that God's Spirit is always with you. Then, even if you're headed to a dreaded dentist appointment, you'll be able to see the little blessings that God sends your way as you look for Him.

God, please help me choose to see each day and each moment as a gift. Change my attitude to be like Yours.

I Love You

*As the Father has loved me, so have I loved you.
Now remain in my love.*

JOHN 15:9 NIV

. . . .

Today is a day to focus completely on the love that God has for you. There is such great joy in knowing that the God of the universe knows us personally and loves us lavishly. Lavish is an adjective *and* a verb. It means "to give without limit." First John 3:1 says "See what great love the Father has lavished on us, that we should be called children of God! And that is what we are!" If you know nothing else about God, know this: God loves you without limit! Remember this as you start your day and brush your teeth. Thank Him for His love as you ride to your next destination. Share this with the ones you love and your friends at church or school. God says: *I LOVE YOU!* Can you hear Him?

God, thank You for Your lavish love. I can't begin to understand how You can know me so personally and still love me without limit! I love You, God. I love You so very much!

A Fearless Life

There is no fear in love. But perfect love drives out fear,
because fear has to do with punishment. The one who
fears is not made perfect in love.

1 JOHN 4:18 NIV

There are a lot of people who live in fear. You see these people every day and you might not know what they struggle with on the inside. They are at church, at school, and at the mall. They might even say they follow God but their lives show more fear than faith. These people fear the future and anything unknown. They worry about their bank accounts, and they fear they won't have enough to make it. The Bible says that we can all live our lives without any fear! His perfect love actually casts it out. Jesus wants us to come to Him with the faith of a child (see Matthew 19:14)! That means coming to Him without any fear and fully trusting that He will do what He promises. You have the Spirit of God in your heart right now reminding you that you don't have to fear. You have freedom to live a joyful, fearless life.

God, thank You that You are with me
and that I never have to be afraid.

Your Smile Makes God Smile!

Charm is deceptive, and beauty does not last;
but a woman who fears the Lord will be greatly praised.
PROVERBS 31:30 NLT

Do you ever wish you looked just a little bit more like a movie star? Or maybe you have green eyes and you've always wanted blue. Or maybe your braces won't come off for one more year and you absolutely hate to smile. Cheer up, dear one. When God looks at you, He smiles! He created you just the way you are with special traits and gifts that only you can use to serve Him! The Bible says that people look at outward appearance but God looks at the heart (see 1 Samuel 16:7). A truly beautiful person shines from the inside out. You've seen the movies! Actresses who are really beautiful but have a mean personality aren't loved for very long. By the end of the movie you can hardly stand them! Their bad attitude makes them look ugly even though they have beautiful features. So give everyone a great big smile— braces or not! Your beauty comes from the inside out. A great smile brightens everyone's day and warms the heart of God. After all, making God smile is all that really matters.

God, help my beauty to come from inside,
and let my smile make someone else happy today, too.

Joy in the Morning

*Weeping may last through the night,
but joy comes with the morning.*
PSALM 30:5 NLT

The Bible reminds us again and again that there are different seasons in life. Just like we have winter, spring, summer, and fall—each bringing something new and necessary to our world—we also have different seasons of life. God's Word tells us that "There is a time for everything, and a season for every activity under the heavens" (Ecclesiastes 3:1).You may be in a hard season of life right now, going through a lot of changes. Yet always remember, it's just a season. You've probably heard the saying: "This, too, shall pass." Allow these thoughts to bring you comfort. The hard stuff might last for a season, but joy is just around the corner.

God, please help me to get through hard days knowing that this is only a season and that You offer constant peace and joy in Your presence. Thank You for the different seasons of my life. Use them to make me more like You.

A New Day

The steadfast love of the LORD never ceases; his mercies never come to an end; they are new every morning; great is your faithfulness.
LAMENTATIONS 3:22–23 ESV

What a great scripture to memorize! God's love never ends. . .and neither does His mercy. Do you know what *mercy* means? Mercy is the true fact that God doesn't punish us as our sins deserve. Grace is when God gives us something that we don't deserve (like forgiveness and special blessings). Mercy is when God chooses *not* to give us something we do deserve (punishment for sin). He does this because of what Jesus did for us on the cross. The Bible tells us that God's mercies are new every morning. So if you feel like you've made a bunch of mistakes today, talk to God about them. Ask Him to forgive you and give you a pure heart. Then go to sleep in peace knowing that our great God forgives you and loves you. God is always ready to give you a fresh start.

Thank You, God, for a fresh start each day. Even when others hold grudges against me sometimes, You never do. Thank You for giving me hope in a new day. Help me to follow You with my whole heart today.

God Is Great

*Sing to GOD, everyone and everything! Get out his salvation
news every day! Publish his glory among the godless
nations, his wonders to all races and religions. And why?
Because GOD is great—well worth praising! No god or
goddess comes close in honor. All the popular gods are stuff
and nonsense, but GOD made the cosmos! Splendor and
majesty flow out of him, strength and joy fill his place.*

1 CHRONICLES 16:23–27 MSG

Start the day with God's Word on your heart. Remember
who He is and what He's done. If you go to a public school
and have friends that aren't believers, you know already
that there are tons of different beliefs out there. People
make up their own gods these days. A god or idol can be
anything that someone worships with their time and attention. The difference is that our God is a living and active
God. He still performs wonders and miracles every single
day. Do you know where to look for them? Ask for God to
give you eyes to see His wondrous miracles and blessings
all around you. . .then watch and trust that He is working in
your life.

*God, You are great. You are worthy of all of my attention.
Open my eyes to see You at work in my heart.*

When You've Lost Your Joy

*"This day is holy to our Lord. Do not grieve,
for the joy of the LORD is your strength."*

NEHEMIAH 8:10 NIV

Have you ever felt completely worn out? So tired of "drama" that you just want to go away and hide for awhile? Or maybe your season of change and hard times is lasting a little too long and you simply can't find any joy right now? Sometimes those feelings cause us to lose our joy in God. The problem with that is that when we lose our joy in loving and serving God, we lose our strength. The Bible says that the joy of the Lord *is* our strength! So when we can't find joy in our relationship with God, we'll run out of strength completely. What can you do about it? Ask God to supernaturally fill you with His joy once again. God can give you His strength to live life with joy again, even in a long, difficult season.

God, will you please fill me with Your joy again? I'm afraid I may have lost it. Please give me Your strength and put a new song in my heart. I want to live a joyful life in You.

God's Rules Bring Joy

The precepts of the LORD are right, giving joy to the heart.
The commands of the LORD are radiant,
giving light to the eyes.

PSALM 19:8 NIV

God doesn't give us rules to make us unhappy. He doesn't tell us right and wrong so that we'll be miserable our entire lives. Just like a wise mother sets rules and good boundaries for her children, so God has given us rules to help us enjoy life better and keep us from danger. In fact, the Bible says that God's rules give joy to our hearts and light to our eyes! When we follow God with all of our hearts, He leads us where He wants us to go. Proverbs 3:6 (NLT) says to "Seek his will in all you do, and he will show you which path to take." This is the best way to live!

God, I thank You for giving me rules to follow.
I know it's because You love me and want to keep me
from danger. Help me to respect Your rules and enjoy
following them. I want my life to make You smile.

Be Sunshine

For at one time you were darkness, but now you are light in the Lord. Walk as children of light.
EPHESIANS 5:8 ESV

Do you know anybody who looks like sunshine? You know, when they walk into the room it's almost like the whole place lights up? Jesus said, "I am the light of the world. Whoever follows me will not walk in darkness, but will have the light of life" (John 8:12 NIV). When we follow Christ Jesus, He fills us up with His very own light. It's the light of life that makes believers shine from the inside out—kinda like sunshine! After a long, cold winter. . . there's nothing like walking out into the sunshine come spring. The sun makes us feel warm, and we actually need the vitamin D the sun provides to be healthy! Ask God to make you into a living sunshine. Ask Him to fill you with His light so that others feel warm and healthy when they are around you. Those are the kind of people that change the world.

God, I want to be sunshine to other people. Fill me to overflowing with Your light and love. Help others to feel the warmth and health that You offer when I walk into a room. . .all for Your glory.

A Walking Bible

I'm thanking you, GOD, from a full heart, I'm writing the book on your wonders. I'm whistling, laughing, and jumping for joy; I'm singing your song, High God.

PSALM 9:1–2 MSG

. . . .

Have you heard the saying "You are the only Bible that some people will ever read"? That means that some people you'll meet during this lifetime have never opened a Bible. Yet God put them in your path so that you can be a living, breathing example of God's Word. Are you writing the book of God's wonders in your life? Not literally. . .you don't really have to write a book. You can *be* the book! When you live out a life of joy and thankfulness. . .other people are going to wonder what is different about you. They're going to want to know why you're full of joy. They'll want to know where you get your joy! That makes you a real-life walking Bible to someone else. You have an amazing opportunity each and every day to make a difference in the lives of everyone you meet. You can make a difference at school, at church, at the library, at the mall, at a restaurant. . .everywhere. The only smile that person might see the whole day could be from you.

God, help me make a difference in someone's life today.

The Greatest Joy

The LORD is compassionate and gracious, slow to anger,
abounding in love.... For as high as the heavens are above
the earth, so great is his love for those who fear him;
as far as the east is from the west, so far has
he removed our transgressions from us.

PSALM 103:8, 11–12 NIV

God doesn't treat us as our sins deserve. He is compassionate. He is gracious. Because of Jesus' work on the cross, He's not angry with us! Instead, He is abounding in love. He sees us as Jesus sees us: *paid for!* Our sins have been obliterated. Theologian J. I. Packer said there is "great incentive to worship and love God in the thought that, for some unfathomable reason, He wants me as His friend, and desires to be my friend, and has given His Son to die for me in order to realize this purpose."

No matter how many times you've messed up, God loves you and desires to be your friend. We have the greatest joy in knowing that because of Jesus, God doesn't hold our sins against us. We are free and dearly loved.

My greatest joy is knowing You, God. I'm so glad
You want me as Your friend!

Strength and Peace

The Lord gives his people strength.
The Lord blesses them with peace.
PSALM 29:11 NLT

. . . .

When we worship the Lord, He gives us His strength and peace. Second Corinthians 1:21–22 (NIV) says, "Now it is God who makes both us and you stand firm in Christ. He anointed us, set his seal of ownership on us, and put his Spirit in our hearts as a deposit, guaranteeing what is to come." How powerful! God has put His very own Spirit in our hearts—the Holy Spirit! He makes us stand firm in Christ. We are His. We have a guarantee of what is to come! Are you longing for strength and peace? God wants to bless you with that. Come before God in the quietness of your heart and talk to Him. Tell Him your thoughts, your wants and needs; tell Him if you're feeling bad about something or if you need an answer about something that's bothering You. God is listening, and He is always available.

God, thank You that You are always listening and available. Help me not to take that for granted. Thank You for Your Spirit inside me. Please fill me with Your strength and peace. Change me to be more like You.

Understanding for Each Moment

Your word is a lamp for my feet, a light on my path. . .
The unfolding of your words gives light;
it gives understanding to the simple.

PSALM 119:105, 130 NIV

God's Word is a lamp for our feet. Reading and knowing God's Word provides us with light so our feet know the next steps to take. We are to obey God step by step and moment by moment. Even when we don't understand what He's doing. Even when obedience doesn't make any sense. Remember the scriptures about God giving us rules and guidance for a reason (see Psalm 19:8)? He has purpose in everything He does and in everything He asks for you to do. God promises it's all for your good and for His glory (see Romans 8:28)! But. . . If God shared all of the details with us up front, we would most likely run the other way. There are some life lessons we all have to learn that aren't easy and fun. God lights up our path just enough so that we can see how to obey Him, step by step and moment by moment.

God, I don't always understand everything You're doing in my life, but I trust You. Help me to get into Your Word and know You better in each moment.

The Peace of Christ

*Peace I leave with you; my peace I give you.
I do not give to you as the world gives.
Do not let your hearts be troubled and do not be afraid.*

JOHN 14:27 NIV

Many people believe that peace means everything is perfect and nothing is going wrong in your life. That idea is not what the Bible teaches. Jesus gives us true peace. When you experience the true peace that only comes from Christ you experience a deep knowing that no matter what happens to you or what is going wrong in your world, God is still in control. This type of peace is the peace that goes beyond what our human minds can understand. This verse tells us that Jesus doesn't give to us as the world gives to us. When we receive something from someone here on earth, these gifts usually don't last for very long and they sometimes have strings attached. The gift of peace from the Lord is eternal and available to all of us who call Him our Savior.

*Dear Jesus, thank You for giving me Your peace
that is beyond what I can understand. Help me not
to be afraid in times of trouble, but to remember
that You are always with me.*

Rise above the Storms

*Then Peter got down out of the boat, walked on the water
and came toward Jesus. But when he saw the wind, he was
afraid and, beginning to sink, cried out, "Lord, save me!"*

MATTHEW 14:29–30 NIV

When our eyes are focused on Christ in worship, we rise
above the storms of life. Like Peter, when we get distracted
and scared by the waves around us, we start to sink. Peter
cried out to God for help when he realized how crazy and
unbelievable it was to step out in faith! The Bible says that
"immediately Jesus reached out his hand and caught him"
(Matthew 14:31 NIV). Are you having trouble stepping out
in faith? Are you sinking in the storms of life? Ask God to
reach out His hand and catch you. Ask Him to forgive you
for doubting. Keep your eyes focused on Him and He will
give you strength and peace in all situations.

*God, sometimes I'm scared to step out in faith and do
the things You ask me to. I forget to keep my eyes on You
and I look at everyone else instead. I feel embarrassed
sometimes. Please forgive me for that and give me
the faith to do Your will.*

True, Lasting Peace

*Don't worry about anything; instead, pray about everything.
Tell God what you need, and thank him for all he has done.
Then you will experience God's peace, which exceeds
anything we can understand. His peace will guard your
hearts and minds as you live in Christ Jesus.*
PHILIPPIANS 4:6-7 NLT

God doesn't just tell us to do something and leave it at
that. He shows us how to do it, and He always has purpose.
God clearly tells us not to worry. We know that's easier said
than done. . .but He asks us to replace worry with prayer!
We can do that! We can! We can even talk to God about
what we're worried about and thank Him for what He has
done and what He will do. That's when He supernaturally
changes our worries into peace. This is a true and lasting
peace. . .not just a feel-good moment.

*God, I pray that Your peace will guard my heart and my
mind. Help me to replace worry with thankfulness.
I trust You to give me true, lasting peace when I do that.
Thank You for loving me so much!*

Keeping the Peace

Turn away from evil and do good. Search for peace, and work to maintain it. The eyes of the LORD watch over those who do right; his ears are open to their cries for help.

PSALM 34:14–15 NLT

Peace isn't easy to come by. Then when we have it, the Bible tells us to work to maintain it. When we obey God by being thankful and not worrying, He gives us that true and lasting peace. It doesn't stay like that forever! We have to keep giving our worries to God and replacing them with thankfulness. . .every. . .single. . .day. It's definitely not just a one-time thing. If we want God to watch over us and hear our prayers, we've got to keep away from evil and do good. The Bible says that we need to turn away from evil. . .to actually stop and go the other direction. We can't just assume that trouble won't find us if we're not looking for it. Our enemy is constantly looking for ways to get us to turn away from God (see 1 Peter 5:8) and destroy our peace. Ask God to help you turn and go the other way so you can keep your eyes on Christ.

God, please help me to turn away from evil and to seek You in all things.

Peace with God and Others

Do all that you can to live in peace with everyone.
ROMANS 12:18 NLT

. . . .

There are definitely days where you might not feel like living at peace with everyone. Maybe you didn't sleep well and you wake up grumpy. Or maybe you had a bad dream that you can't stop thinking about and it's bothering you. Or maybe you have no idea why you are annoyed—you just are—and you want people to leave you alone for awhile. The best thing to do when you feel like that is to find a quiet place just to be with God. Ask your friends and family to give you a little space and go talk to God about the way you're feeling. Even if you don't understand why you feel the way you do. . .God does! So take your problems to Him first and allow Him to help you sort them out. Ask Him to change your attitude as He works on your heart. Then you can enjoy peaceful relationships with others because you know that the God who created you is working on your problems with you.

God, sometimes I can get pretty grumpy with other people. Please forgive me for that and help me to take my thoughts and feelings to You first.

Guiding Me

Send out your light and your truth; let them lead me;
let them bring me to your holy hill and to your dwelling!
PSALM 43:3 ESV

. . . .

Moment by moment God is with you and available to
guide you through any and every situation. He wants to
be happy along with you during good times. He wants to
comfort you during times of sadness. He wants to guide
you and give you peace through times of confusion and
decision-making. Psalm 73:24 (NIV) says, "You guide me
with your counsel, and afterward you will take me into
glory." Jesus promised that the Holy Spirit would come
and guide us in all truth (see John 16:13). God will guide
us as we listen to His Spirit for wisdom during this life,
and then He'll take us to heaven. When we give our lives
to Christ, the Holy Spirit miraculously comes to live inside
of us and we are no longer alone. We don't have to figure
things out by ourselves. We don't have to stress like those
who have no purpose in life. God's Spirit is always with us.

God, thanks for being with me in every single moment.
Fill me with Your Spirit today and help me
to be listening for Your guidance.

God's Will

"But the Advocate, the Holy Spirit, whom the Father will send in my name, will teach you all things and will remind you of everything I have said to you."

JOHN 14:26 NIV

Do you feel like you have a ton of decisions to make right now? Sometimes life gets pretty confusing. Yet the Bible tells us that "God is not a God of confusion but of peace" (1 Corinthians 14:33 ESV). He doesn't want you to be confused but have peace that He has Your future in His hands. He knows exactly where you're going to be ten years from now and exactly what you'll be doing. When you feel confused and you want to know God's will, just ask! God's Spirit inside you will teach you and show you His will as you seek Him in each moment. Get into God's Word and you'll get to know His will even better. A great verse to keep in mind is Jeremiah 29:11. God knows the plans He has for you and they are to give you a hope and a future.

God, help me make decisions that honor You. Please give me the desire to get into Your Word and know You more.

A Peaceful Heart

A peaceful heart leads to a healthy body;
jealousy is like cancer in the bones.
PROVERBS 14:30 NLT

When you wake up each morning, ask God to give you a peaceful heart. Ask Him to look into your heart and clean out anything that does not honor Him. If you are hiding jealousy or bitterness toward someone else in your heart, the Bible tells us that doing so can be as dangerous for your body as cancer! Did you know that? Constant stress is very difficult on the body; scientists have been studying the effects of high stress for many years. Holding onto bitterness or jealousy causes stress on your body, and it keeps your heart from being clean before God. However, having a peaceful heart starts with bringing everything—all your thoughts and feelings—before God and asking Him to make them match up with His plan and purpose for you. Your heart and the rest of your body will thank you for it! (P. S. So will your friends and family!)

Dear God, please give me a peaceful heart today. Is there
anything I'm holding onto that doesn't honor You? Please
show me so that I can live a life that pleases You.

Perfect Peace

You will keep in perfect peace all who trust in you,
all whose thoughts are fixed on you!
ISAIAH 26:3 NLT

. . . .

The Bible talks about taking every thought captive (see 2 Corinthians 10:5). Do you know what that means and why it is so very important? Perfect peace happens only in the presence of God. It doesn't mean that nothing bad will ever happen to you. It means that whenever something happens to you—good, bad, boring, etc.—take it immediately to God. Talk to Him about it. He will give you peace for each moment that you share with Him. Wouldn't it be great to live out your life in perfect peace? Well. . .you can! If you're waiting at the dentist's office bored or nervous, talk to God. If you are on your way to Disney World and can hardly contain your excitement, talk to God. If you are sad about losing a friend or loved one, talk to God. He offers perfect peace in every moment for anyone who fixes their thoughts on Him!

God, I really do want to live my life in perfect peace with You. Please help me to remember You in all things and all situations. Thank You that You are constantly with me!

Life and Peace

*So letting your sinful nature control your mind leads
to death. But letting the Spirit control your mind
leads to life and peace.*

ROMANS 8:6 NLT

You have a big choice to make today. Life and death are at stake. You can allow the Spirit to take over. . .or allow your sinful nature to do all the talking. Our sinful nature gets us into all kinds of trouble. When we allow our own nature to control us we gossip, we do what we want without considering others. Often we hurt others. We sometimes lie and cheat, and we forget about God's Spirit in our hearts. However, when we allow the Spirit of God to take over. . .we seek the things that God seeks: love, joy, peace, patience, kindness, goodness, faithfulness, and self-control. Those things lead to life and peace. Which will you choose today?

God, today I choose to lay down my own desires and let Your Spirit take control. It's so amazing to me that Your Spirit actually lives inside my heart! Help me to never forget or ignore that! I want to seek the things that You want.

Let Peace Rule

*And let the peace that comes from Christ rule in your
hearts. For as members of one body you are called
to live in peace. And always be thankful.*
COLOSSIANS 3:15 NLT

When you have a thankful heart, peace can rule. When you
have an unhappy and bitter heart, there is no place for anything else. Remember, it's always your own choice. Sure,
you can't control a lot of the things that happen to you
right now—like where you live or where you go to school—
but you can control your attitude about it. You can choose
to be thankful that you have a place to sleep each night in
a warm bed. There are 1.6 million children that are home-
less right here in the United States! You can choose to be
thankful that you know how to read and write. There are
millions of children in the world that have to work instead
of going to school and may never learn how to read. Your
life might not be exactly the way you want it right now,
but you can still choose to be thankful and let the peace of
Christ rule in your heart.

*Thank You, God, for everything I have. Help me to choose
thankfulness even when I don't feel like it.*

Chasing After the Right Stuff

*So flee youthful passions and pursue righteousness,
faith, love, and peace, along with those who
call on the Lord from a pure heart.*

2 TIMOTHY 2:22 ESV

You probably know some people your age who are chasing after all kinds of things: money, clothes, electronics, and a lot of other "things" that don't really matter. Some young people think they'll only be happy if they have a boyfriend or girlfriend. Here's the truth: chasing after all of that will never fill you up and make you truly happy. Only God can meet the deep longings in our hearts. He wants us to chase after right living. He wants us to choose to trust Him and pursue love and peace. Our self-image should never be based on the things we have or on other people. You might be transferred to a new school and not know a single soul, but you can still be the happiest person in the building because of the faith, love, and peace that are ruling in your heart.

God, please help me to remember that things don't really matter and they don't have to affect the way I feel about myself. Help me put my trust and confidence in You alone.

Peace in Every Situation

Now may the Lord of peace himself give you his peace at all times and in every situation. The Lord be with you all.
2 THESSALONIANS 3:16 NLT

Remember the scripture about taking every thought captive? Here's a reminder: "We demolish arguments and every pretension that sets itself up against the knowledge of God, and we take captive every thought to make it obedient to Christ" (2 Corinthians 10:5 NIV). The apostle Paul wrote these words to some of the first Christians because some false teachers were saying things that weren't true about God. God tells us what to do about that through the words of Paul. He says for us to match everything someone else says or does with God's Word. That's how we'll know if it's true or not. If someone says or does something you think isn't good, go talk to God about it and get in His Word. Don't believe everything you hear—even if someone thinks they know more about God than you do. You have the right to go to God about everything all by yourself. That's how God can give you peace at all times and in every situation.

Thank You, God, that I can always come to You about everything.

Troubles Bring Patience

We continue to shout our praise even when we're hemmed in with troubles, because we know how troubles can develop passionate patience in us.

ROMANS 5:3 MSG

When you're going through some hard times, it's easy to get discouraged. You want things to change, and you want them to change quickly! Sometimes it can be really hard to keep a good attitude when you need things to change so badly. Yet hard times can actually be really, really good things if we allow God to work in them. We learn to trust God more in times of trouble. Hard times teach us to be patient, too. Hard things give us an opportunity to trust God's Word. We remember Romans 8:28 (NIV) that says, "We know that in all things God works for the good of those who love him, who have been called according to his purpose." We patiently trust God to bring good out of bad.

God, I know I can give You praise and thank You even during hard times. I trust Your Word, and I choose to wait patiently and watch with great expectation while You turn these bad things into good life lessons.

The Four Soils

*As for that in the good soil, they are those who,
hearing the word, hold it fast in an honest
and good heart, and bear fruit with patience.*
LUKE 8:15 ESV

. . . .

Have you ever read the story of the soils? Jesus tells a
parable in Luke 8 about a farmer that goes out to plant
seeds. Some seed fell on the path, some on the rock, some
on thorns, and some on good soil. The only seed that grew
into a big crop was the seed that fell on good soil. Jesus
explained this parable to His followers so they would know
what He meant. The seed that produced the good crop
stood for people who heard God's Word and followed Him
no matter what. They patiently trusted God for all things
and God blessed them for it. Read the rest of Luke 8 and
learn about the other kinds of soil. Which one are you?

*God, I want to be like the seed that fell on the good soil.
Please make my heart open to hear Your Word and to put
it into practice. I pray that You will bless my life
and let me be a blessing to others.*

Be Still and Wait

Be still before the LORD and wait patiently for him;
do not fret when people succeed in their ways,
when they carry out their wicked schemes.
PSALM 37:7 NIV

Be still and wait. . .some of the hardest words for us to
hear and sometimes nearly impossible for us to do! God
wants us to come before him and wait patiently as He does
His will in our lives. He tells us not to worry when bad
things happen, because He will make all things right. In
fact, Jesus said "It is finished!" as He was hanging on the
cross. That means that death and sin have been conquered
forever! They have no hold on us. Bad people might do bad
things and seemingly get away with it for now, but God
sees all things and everything is in His hands. So the next
time someone does something mean to you on purpose,
go straight to God and be still. Don't take out your own
revenge. Just wait patiently for God to take care of it. It
sounds hard, but God will give you the strength to do
things His way.

God, please give me the strength to take matters to You
instead of taking them into my own hands. Help me
to be patient and wait for You.

Patience Calms a Quarrel

A hot-tempered person stirs up conflict,
but the one who is patient calms a quarrel.
PROVERBS 15:18 NIV

You may know some people who just love to argue. They really don't care much about other people's feelings. . .they just want to be right. So they have a lot to say, and they rarely ever listen. This is the kind of person who stirs up trouble. A patient person, on the other hand, cares more about the other person and is very good at listening. This is the kind of person you want for a friend. If you have someone in your family who stirs up trouble, pray for that person. Ask God to step in and soften their heart. Sometimes they don't even know how much they hurt people. Ask God to show them. Work on being a patient person who lights up other people's lives.

God, please forgive me for the times that I've picked a fight
with someone else. Help me to be a patient person who
listens and cares for others. Help me to light up the lives of
people around me. I want to point them to You.

Hope, Patience, and Prayer

Be joyful in hope, patient in affliction, faithful in prayer.
ROMANS 12:12 NIV

Author and pastor Max Lucado says, "God meets daily needs daily. Not weekly or annually. He will give you what you need when it is needed." Trusting God to meet our needs helps us to be joyful as we put our hope and trust in God. We can trust that God sees us and knows exactly what we need when we need it. Isn't that amazing? The God of creation sees *you* and knows exactly what you need right at this very moment. So we can be patient when things seem tough because we believe God will meet our needs (see Philippians 4:19). God also wants us to be faithful in prayer. Pray for God to give you a clean heart and to show you where you've messed up, and thank Him for forgiving you. Talk to God about all of your needs and thoughts. Also ask God to care for those around you. Prayer changes things! The Bible tells us that when our hearts are right with God, our prayers are powerful and effective (see James 5:16)!

*Thank You, God, for hearing my prayers
and meeting all of my needs.*

Love Is Patient

Love is patient, love is kind. It does not envy,
it does not boast, it is not proud.
1 CORINTHIANS 13:4 NIV

You'll meet a lot of people in this world who have no idea
what true love is. True love is nothing like what you see
in the movies. Our enemy has confused the world into
thinking that love equals affection (or nice feelings), but
that simply isn't true. Love is a choice and it is not really
a feeling at all! We can actually love someone without
liking them very much. For example, when someone at
school talks behind your back. . .you can respond without
hurting them back. That is a loving action. . .even if you
don't like that person very much. Or maybe you have
a friend and you're trying to help them with their home-
work but they just aren't getting it. You can respond by
being patient instead of getting frustrated. Check out
1 Corinthians 13. This chapter in the Bible gives us a
clear picture of what true love looks like.

Dear God, please help me to understand what true love is.
Help me choose to love people no matter how I might feel
about them. Thank You that You love me no
matter what. Help me love like that!

The Spirit of God in Me

Be completely humble and gentle; be patient,
bearing with one another in love.
EPHESIANS 4:2 NIV

The dictionary defines the word *humble* as: "not proud or arrogant." It means you're not full of yourself and that you're not a show-off. God wants us to be humble and gentle people. . .like Jesus. Jesus had every reason to be a show-off—He was God! Yet He was humble and lived His life to serve others. Being humble and gentle doesn't mean that you are timid and shy, though. Remember that the Spirit of God lives inside of you! This means that the very same power that rose Jesus up from the grave is the power that is living in you. God gave us this power to love Him and love others well. It takes extraordinary power to be humble, gentle, and patient. . .especially when you don't feel like it. Ask God to open your eyes to His power that is alive inside of you—and use that power to love like Jesus loved.

Please open my eyes to Your Spirit, God. I've asked You
into my life so I know that Your power is readily available
to me. Help me to love others well. . .like You do.

Looking for the Best

*Be patient with each person, attentive to individual needs.
And be careful that when you get on each other's nerves you
don't snap at each other. Look for the best in each other,
and always do your best to bring it out.*

1 THESSALONIANS 5:14–15 MSG

Even the best of friends get on each other's nerves sometimes. Have you ever gone to summer camp with your best
friend and shared a cabin? By the end of the week, friends
can get easily annoyed with each other because they don't
have enough space. Brothers and sisters seem to get on
our nerves the most! They never leave us alone! What is
the best thing to do? Find a quiet place and talk to God
first. Ask Him to change your heart again. Then remember all the good things you like about your friend or your
sibling. If you know something you do really annoys them?
Try not to do it so much! Be patient with people and look
for the best in them.

*God, please help me to take a time-out when I'm annoyed at
other people. Change my heart and help me to be patient.
Help me to look for the best in others.*

Steady and Strong

*Meanwhile, friends, wait patiently for the Master's Arrival.
You see farmers do this all the time, waiting for their
valuable crops to mature, patiently letting the rain do its
slow but sure work. Be patient like that. Stay steady and
strong. The Master could arrive at any time.*

JAMES 5:7 MSG

The Bible tells us that Jesus is coming back to take us with
Him to heaven (see John 14:1-4). Jesus' second coming
could happen at any moment. No one knows the day or
the hour. While we wait for His return, God wants us to
be steady and strong. A lot of things will happen in our
lifetime that can lead us astray. The enemy is actually
looking for ways to get you to turn away from God. When
that happens, turn to God and His strength. Ask for His
supernatural power to work in you as you patiently wait for
Christ to come. Is your heart right with God? Those who
follow Christ don't have to worry. Those who haven't trusted
Christ should be afraid. Jesus is coming back soon!

*God, please help me to be steady and strong as I wait
patiently for Your return. Help me to be a loving witness for
You so that my friends can be with You for all eternity, too.*

The Coming of Jesus

God isn't late with his promise as some measure lateness.
He is restraining himself on account of you, holding back
the End because he doesn't want anyone lost. He's giving
everyone space and time to change.

Many people wonder why Jesus hasn't come back already.
I mean, isn't this world messed up enough? Isn't it about
time for God to remove all the bad stuff from this world?
Peter has an answer for that. God loves us so much, and He
doesn't want to send anyone to eternal judgment. He wants
everyone to trust Him. So, He is patient. . .giving people
more time than they deserve to make a choice for Christ.
Remember, what seems like an eternity to us is really just
a few short days to God. The Bible says a day is like a
thousand years and a thousand years are like a day to God
(see Psalm 90:4; 2 Peter 3:8). So continue to ask for divine
patience and live like Jesus could come back today!

I'm so thankful You have saved me, Lord. I'm waiting
patiently for You to return. Please give me strength and
patience as I tell my friends and family about You,
and help me to live each day like today might be the day!

Wise and Patient

A person's wisdom yields patience;
it is to one's glory to overlook an offense.
PROVERBS 19:11 NIV

A wise person is a patient person who isn't easily offended. This doesn't mean that a wise person allows other people to walk all over them like a doormat. It just means that wise people aren't overly sensitive. . .they don't overanalyze everything that other people say to them or about them. Wouldn't it be great to not worry about what other people think about you. . .or what they may be saying about you behind your back? Well. . .guess what? You don't have to! The only person you ever need to please with all your heart and soul is God. You don't have to worry about what anyone else thinks of you as long as your heart is right with God. God doesn't want us to be people-pleasers. . .He wants us to be Jesus-pleasers!

God, I wish I had more wisdom. Will You please help me to
make better choices based on truth? I want to make wise
decisions and to honor You with my life. Help me to
concern myself with pleasing You alone and not with
worrying about what anyone else thinks.

Take Heart

Wait for the LORD; be strong and take heart
and wait for the LORD.
PSALM 27:14 NIV

. . . .

When you're feeling stressed about something, the best thing to do is to take the issue straight to God. You don't need to call a friend for advice, just go straight to God about it. Going to a trusted friend or parent is always a good thing, but it really should be the second thing we do in any situation. God is always with us and ready to help. We forget this so many times! He wants to lead us and give us peace in every situation. The Bible tells us that we can always approach the throne of God with confidence. He will give us grace and mercy in our time of need (see Hebrews 4:16).

The next time you're tempted to call a friend before talking to God. . .stop yourself and quiet your heart before God. Wait for Him to lead you. Be strong and take heart. . . because God is in control, and He has the whole situation in His hands.

God, please help me to run to You first, before I seek out advice from others. I want to automatically come to You before anyone else. Thank You that I can come to Your throne confidently because of what Jesus did for me on the cross.

In a Hurry

I wait for the LORD, my soul waits, and in his word I hope.
PSALM 130:5 ESV

We seem to always be in a hurry on this earth. It's a rush to get to school or church on time, then practice, then the game, and then to piano practice or sports practice number two. . .we are running, running, running. It's okay to have lots of activities as long as we make sure we still have time for God. Did you know that God took a rest after He created the first week? The Bible says He blessed that day and made it holy (see Genesis 2:1). Did the God of all creation need a rest? No, He is God! Yet He rested as an example for us to follow. God wants us to rest from our work and our activities. He wants us to create space for Him in our lives.

God, sometimes I'm not very good at resting and creating space for You in my life. Would You please help me with that? Show me how to live a better life. A life that honors Your Word and keeps my body healthy.

Set Out to Do Good

Whoever pursues righteousness and kindness
will find life, righteousness, and honor.

PROVERBS 21:21 ESV

. . . .

Do you pursue righteousness and kindness? Kindness is a pretty simple act. Most of us understand how to be kind and that everyone likes to be treated with kindness. What does pursuing righteousness mean? The God's Word translation of the Bible explains that pursuing righteousness means that you're seeking God's approval (see Philippians 3:9). We can't do that on our own. The only way to receive God's approval is through accepting what Jesus did for us on the cross and living for Him. When we've done that, God looks at us and sees us through Jesus! That means He sees us as perfect and nothing we could ever do or not do could make Him love us any more than He already does! Think about that today! If you want to find life, righteousness, and honor. . .live for Jesus and act out of kindness.

God, thank You again and again for Your great love for me.
I'm so thankful that Jesus took away all of my sin—
past, present, and future. Please give me the desire
to seek You all the days of my life!

A Noble Woman

*She opens her mouth with wisdom,
and the teaching of kindness is on her tongue.*
PROVERBS 31:26 ESV

Comic strip writer Scott Adams said "Remember there's no such thing as a small act of kindness. Every act creates a ripple with no logical end." So every time you treat someone else with kindness, you bless that person. Then that person may go on to bless someone else. . .and they bless someone else. . .and on and on! That is such an amazing thought! The Proverbs 31 woman knew this. The Bible gives us a great example for a godly woman in the book of Proverbs. You may not be able to do all of the things this woman does, but God gives us all gifts and personalities that we can use to bless others. Kindness is one of them. If you desire to grow up and be a woman of God, check out the Proverbs 31 woman. Ask God to show you what gifts He has given you to bless other people. One act of kindness passed on and on and on. . .can change the world!

*God, please help me to use my personality
and gifts to be a blessing to others.*

God's Kindness

The LORD appeared to us in the past, saying:
"I have loved you with an everlasting love;
I have drawn you with unfailing kindness."

JEREMIAH 31:3 NIV

Many people grow up with some knowledge of who God is. Many people get it wrong. They might believe that He is the Creator of the world, but they also think He is a grumpy man sitting at the edge of heaven just waiting to zap each of us when we fail. Nothing could be further from the truth. This verse in Jeremiah gives us a true picture of who God is. He has loved each of us with an everlasting love, and His kindness is unfailing! God is good, and He is kind! He doesn't smother you with shame when you mess up; He gently convicts you and draws you back to repentance with His love and kindness (see Romans 2:4). He is a holy God worthy of all of our respect and honor, but He is not mean or grouchy.

God, I'm sorry that I've had a wrong idea about who You
are. Help me to get to know the real You. The One who loves
me forever! Thank You for Your amazing kindness to me,
even when I don't deserve it.

Fair, Kind, and Humble

He has told you, O man, what is good; and what does the
LORD require of you but to do justice, and to love kindness,
and to walk humbly with your God?

MICAH 6:8 ESV

In the Old Testament book of Micah, the people of Israel continued to disobey God. They were making really bad choices. . .even building altars to false gods! Yet God was still kind and patient with them. He used a prophet named Micah to remind them of what He wanted them to do. Micah spoke to the people and told them that God wanted them to do justice (to be fair in all of their ways), to be kind, and to walk humbly with God. God is good, and all His ways are good. He wants us to follow Him by making those same kinds of choices. How are you doing at being fair, kind, and humble? Are you walking with God each day. . .or choosing your own way?

God, please help me to walk with You each day in a way
that makes You smile! Help me to be fair and kind,
just like You! Help me to be humble, too.

Show Kindness

And the word of the LORD came to Zechariah, saying,
"Thus says the LORD of hosts, Render true judgments, show
kindness and mercy to one another, do not oppress the widow,
the fatherless, the sojourner, or the poor, and let none of you
devise evil against another in your heart."
ZECHARIAH 7:8-10 ESV

God is kind, and His ways are kind. All through the Bible
you will find examples of God's lovingkindness. One of the
most important character traits that God wants us to have
is kindness. There are still a lot of people in this world
who don't know much about God, or they have the wrong
idea about who God is. It's our job as His followers to show
them who God really is. He wants the very best for us. He
is not out to keep us from having fun. . .just the opposite!
God wants us to have abundant life (see John 10:10) and to
live joy-filled lives. If we live our lives with kindness in our
hearts, the people around us will get a different and true
view of God.

God, help me be a good example of who You are.
Help me to show kindness to everyone so that
they can see You in a different and true way.

The Kindness of God

"Yet he has not left himself without testimony:
He has shown kindness by giving you rain from heaven
and crops in their seasons; he provides you with plenty
of food and fills your hearts with joy."

ACTS 14:17 NIV

The Bible says that every person is without excuse when it comes to knowing if God exists or not. Look outside! Did the grass, trees, and animals just happen by chance? Are babies born by accident? Did we evolve from frogs or apes? Of course not! You are not an accident and neither was anything else that has been created. God gives us rain and vegetables and food. . . . He fills our hearts with joy. Could that just happen by accident? No way. The kindness of God is everywhere. He has purpose in everything He does, and you were created for a purpose, too. Know what it is? To love! God created us in His great kindness to love Him and to love others!

Thank You for Your great kindness to me, God.
I'm so thankful for Your presence in my life. Fill me up
with purpose so that I can live a life of love.

God's Gifts

*Now God has us where he wants us, with all the time
in this world and the next to shower grace and kindness
upon us in Christ Jesus. Saving is all his idea, and all his
work. All we do is trust him enough to let him do it.
It's God's gift from start to finish!*

EPHESIANS 2:7–10 MSG

Do you see God as someone who showers grace and
kindness upon you each day? That's exactly what He wants
to do. He loves you so much that He sent His Son to take
away all the sin from your heart and from everyone else
in the whole world. All you have to do is trust Him! Jesus
is God's great gift to us so that He can shower more and
more gifts upon us. Think of a mother who delights in
getting her little ones special presents for birthdays and
Christmas. She searches and plans to find exactly the
perfect gift to make her child smile. The Bible tells us that
even sinful people know how to give good gifts to their
children so "how much more will your heavenly Father
give good gifts to those who ask him" (Matthew 7:11 NLT).

*Thank You for the gift of Jesus. Thank You
for blessing me over and over again.*

Wear Love

*So, chosen by God for this new life of love, dress in the
wardrobe God picked out for you: compassion, kindness,
humility, quiet strength, discipline. Be even-tempered,
content with second place, quick to forgive an offense.
Forgive as quickly and completely as the Master forgave
you. And regardless of what else you put on, wear love.
It's your basic, all-purpose garment. Never be without it.*
COLOSSIANS 3:12–13 MSG

Did you know that you were chosen by God to live a life
of love? You are chosen and precious and deeply loved by
God! As you pick out your clothes for the day, think about
this verse. You would never leave the house without wearing something that covers your body, right? God wants you
to think the same way about love. He wants you to cover
yourself with love so that you can live a life of love for
God and others. He also gives you some other directions
about how to live: with compassion, kindness, humility,
and discipline. He also wants you to be strong and not lose
your temper. He doesn't want you to be a sore loser when it
comes to competition. What is the most important thing?
Love! If you don't start with love, nothing else matters!

*Help me love better, Lord. If I start with love,
everything else will fall right into place.*

Trust in the Lord and Do Good

*Trust in the LORD, and do good; dwell in the land
and befriend faithfulness.*

PSALM 37:3 ESV

None of us is perfect, and we all make big mistakes from
time to time. Some of us forget God for awhile until we
realize how much we've messed up without Him. First
John 1:9 (NIV) says, "If we confess our sins, he is faithful
and just and will forgive us our sins and purify us from
all unrighteousness." When you've messed up big, turn
back to God; start to trust Him again. . .to *really* trust
Him. When you trust God with everything you have, He
gives you the ability to do good and to be faithful. His
power is alive and at work within you. There is something
very powerful about coming to God and confessing your
sins to Him. He already knows what you've done, but
He wants to talk with you about it. He wants to help you
through it and give you peace. He will give you the
power to trust Him more and to do good.

*God, I know I've messed up big-time. Will You please forgive
me and change my heart? Show me a better way.*

Forgiveness and Goodness

Turn away from evil and do good;
so shall you dwell forever.
PSALM 37:27 ESV

Author and preacher Billy Graham said: "Man has two great spiritual needs. One is for forgiveness. The other is for goodness." We can find both of these in Christ alone. When we confess our sins to Christ and receive His forgiveness, the next step is for us to turn away from the sin we've been involved in. We can't pretend it will just go away on its own. It takes action on our part. We can't find goodness on our own either—we have to let the Spirit of God develop goodness inside of us. That happens when we lay our whole lives down before Him—we confess our sins, we talk to Him about everything, and we listen for His leading in our lives.

God, I really do want to lay my life down before You.
Please keep me from evil and plant goodness in my heart.
I want to do Your will and to bring glory and honor to You.
Please make my life an example of Your love,
forgiveness, and goodness.

Praying for Goodness

*LORD, do good to those who are good,
to those who are upright in heart.*
PSALM 125:4 NIV

. . . .

Remember that the Bible tell us that our prayers are powerful and effective. So it's important to pray about everything
that comes to your mind. You can pray big prayers, too!
In the Old Testament, a man named Jabez prayed a really
big prayer! He prayed: "Oh that you would bless me and
enlarge my territory! Let your hand be with me, and keep
me from harm so that I will be free from pain." You know
what? The Bible says that God granted his request (see 1
Chronicles 4:10)! Prayer can be a mystery. It's important
to remember that God sees all and knows all. Sometimes
something that seems right and good to us isn't the very
best for us from God's perspective. Yet you can still ask
and talk to God about everything you need and desire.
Ask Him to help your prayers line up with His perfect
plan for you.

*God, I have a lot on my mind. I pray that You would bless
me and my family. Help us to do Your will, and help our
desires line up with Yours.*

Goodness Leads to Rewards

Lead good people down a wrong path and you'll come to a bad end; do good and you'll be rewarded for it.
PROVERBS 28:10 MSG

A nineteenth-century American author named Henry David Thoreau once said: "Goodness is the only investment that never fails." The Bible confirms that idea. This Proverb reminds us that if you purposely set out to do harm to someone, it won't end well. Yet if you pursue goodness and you care for others out of love in your heart, you'll be rewarded. God sees all and knows all. He knows if you're doing something just for show or if you actually care about someone else. He knows if you're doing something for attention or if you are doing something to help someone else without wanting anything in return. Goodness. . .true goodness. . .seeks to do good for others without expecting any rewards. That's a kind of goodness you can't fake!

God, help me to be real in my love for You and for others. Please give me the desire to do good to others without expecting anything for it. Help me to truly care about other people and to help them whenever I can.

Be Happy and Do Good

*I know that there is nothing better for people than
to be happy and to do good while they live. That each of
them may eat and drink, and find satisfaction in
all their toil—this is the gift of God.*
ECCLESIASTES 3:12–13 NIV

King Solomon wrote the book of Ecclesiastes to remind
us all that life is meaningless unless we are following God.
He had wealth and power and whatever He wanted. . .but
He admits that it was all worth nothing because He chose
to ignore God for many years. He wrote Ecclesiastes as He
was looking back on his life. You may wish for lots of money
and want a lot of things you don't have, but take a look
at all that Solomon has to say. In Ecclesiastes 3, Solomon
reminds us that God wants us to enjoy life—but with Him
and not apart from Him. Some people think that it's more
fun to ignore God and do whatever they want, but Solomon
knows this is not true. John 10:10 tells us that Jesus came
so that we can have abundant life—a good and joyful life—
here and for all eternity!

*God, remind me that You want me to live a joyful life—
with You always by my side.*

God Is Good

*GOD proves to be good to the man who passionately waits,
to the woman who diligently seeks. It's a good thing to
quietly hope, quietly hope for help from GOD. It's a good
thing when you're young to stick it out through the hard times.*
LAMENTATIONS 3:25–27 MSG

Pastor and author Dr. Charles Stanley said, "If you tell God
no because He won't explain the reason He wants you to
do something, you are actually hindering His blessing. But
when you say yes to Him, all of heaven opens to pour out
His goodness and reward your obedience. What matters
more than material blessings are the things He is teaching
us in our spirit." Have you ever felt God nudging you to do
something? You know, that thought in your head asking
you to do something good for someone else or to go outside of you comfort zone and meet someone else's need?
When you tell God no, you can hinder Him from blessing
you! However, when you say yes, God says yes, too!

*God, please give me the courage to say yes to You! I know
You will help me through anything You ask me to do.*

Go Above and Beyond

And if you do good to those who are good to you,
what credit is that to you? Even sinners do that.
LUKE 6:33 NIV

It's easy to be kind to our friends and family members who are always kind in return. It's easy to love those who love us back. However, God asks us to go above and beyond. He actually asks us to love the unlovable! Maybe you know a really mean person at school. A lot of times that person is mean because someone at home is being mean to him or her. Deep inside, that mean person longs for love and acceptance. Pray for that person. Ask God to show His love to him or her. Ask Him to show you little ways that you can share His love with that person. It might take days, months, or years for a hard heart to soften. . .but don't give up! God is able to do above and beyond what we could ever imagine!

God, help me to love people the way You do. Even the ones
I think I could never love. I pray for the mean kids that
probably have someone else being mean to them.
Help me show Your love in big and small ways.

Do Good to Your Enemies

*But love your enemies, do good to them, and lend to them
without expecting to get anything back. Then your reward
will be great, and you will be children of the Most High,
because he is kind to the ungrateful and wicked.*

LUKE 6:35 NIV

Hopefully you don't have too many enemies at your age,
but the Bible says that people will hate you just because
you believe in God. Don't let this scare you from telling
others that you love God! The important thing is to *show*
them that you love God. Our actions speak a lot louder
than our words. First John 3:18 says: "Dear children, let
us not love with words or speech but with actions and
in truth." People can spot a fake a mile away. So if you're
going to love someone, do it with all your heart—with your
actions. Pray for God to change any false motives that
might be in you, and do good to others without expecting
anything in return.

*God, sometimes it's hard to love people that aren't
very nice. Will You please give me supernatural
strength from You to show true love to others?*

A New Family

*Therefore, as we have opportunity, let us do good to all
people, especially to those who belong
to the family of believers.*

GALATIANS 6:10 NIV

Did you know that when you commit to follow Christ you immediately gain millions of brothers and sisters? God sets us in His family when we commit our lives to Him, so all believers everywhere are our brothers and sisters in Christ. As brothers and sisters, we have a responsibility to each other: to love each other and help each other whenever we can. The amazing thing about this giant new family you've found yourself in is that you now have people all over the world that have your back. They love God, and some of them are even praying for you! Don't forget to pray for your fellow brothers and sisters in Christ serving in their churches, schools, and in foreign countries! Your new family is huge and needs lots of love and encouragement.

*God, thank You for giving me a new family. I pray for my
brothers and sisters in Christ to be encouraged
and to be strong in their faith.*

Make Time for God-Things

*Be very careful, then, how you live—not as unwise
but as wise, making the most of every opportunity,
because the days are evil. Therefore do not be foolish,
but understand what the Lord's will is.*
EPHESIANS 5:15-17 NIV

Is there a chance you're wasting time on things God might
not want you to be doing? You might be spending your
time doing a lot of really great things: service projects,
serving at church or Sunday school, singing in the church
choir, volunteering at soup kitchens, spending time with
the elderly, etc. Yet one person can't possibly do all of
those things all of the time, and believe it or not—God
doesn't ask that of everyone. Sometimes you have to let go
of really good things to make time in your life for the very
best things. *God-things.* Make time for the activities and
projects that *He* has for you. Ask God to show you what is
most important, and spend your time joyfully serving Him
in those areas with all of your heart.

*God, I bring all of my plans and activities to You.
Will You show me the things that You want for me to do?
I want my life and my time to honor You.*

God Created You to Do Good

For we are God's handiwork, created in Christ Jesus to do good works, which God prepared in advance for us to do.
EPHESIANS 2:10 NIV

. . . .

The Creator of all things made you. . .and you are a masterpiece! You are God's handiwork, and everything about you is lovely to Him! If there is something about your body that you don't like, it's almost like you're telling God that He did a bad job. Have you ever thought about that? Thank God for making you, and ask Him to give you His perspective on the way He made you. God created you for a purpose—to love Him and to love others. He has certain things that He specifically created you to do during your time here on earth. If you're walking with God on a daily basis and listening for His guidance in your life, you'll get to know His voice, and you'll be ready to do exactly what He has for you to do.

God, I'm sorry when I get down on myself and worry about the way I look. You are my Creator, and You made me the way I look and with the personality I have to do good works for You. Help me to look to You always for my self-worth.

Replace Judging with Loving

*For in the same way you judge others, you will be judged,
and with the measure you use, it will be measured to you.*
MATTHEW 7:2 NIV

It's not easy to put yourself in someone else's shoes. The Bible warns to be careful when you judge someone. When you judge someone without understanding their situation, you'll often be put in a very similar situation during your lifetime. That's what "the measure you use will be used on you" means. Sometimes, God allows things like that to happen so that you can understand and forgive those toward whom you harbor bitter feelings. The mean girl at school? She might have a really bad home-life and she only knows how to express herself through anger. The boy who smells bad and wears dirty clothes? His dad may have lost his job and they can't afford deodorant. Or maybe their water was even shut off! You just never know. So pray for them, and be careful how you judge them.

*Dear God, please help me not to judge others. I want to be
a loving example of You to everyone I see each day.
Help me not to avoid people I don't understand,
and please give me wisdom to know how
to act around them.*

Paybacks

*See that no one repays anyone evil for evil, but always seek
to do good to one another and to everyone.*
1 THESSALONIANS 5:15 ESV

Have you ever been wrongfully accused? Maybe a kid at
school blamed you for something and the teacher didn't
know who to believe. Or maybe you had a big misunder-
standing with someone and they accused you of lying
when that was never your intention. Stuff like that happens. . .and it hurts. You wish that God would speak up—
right out of the sky—and tell the other person what really
happened! But God promises that He sees and that He will
take care of things in the best way possible. It can be so
hard to keep your anger in check and not try to payback
someone for hurting you. God says to leave the paybacks
to Him (see Romans 12:19). He's the only one who sees
every side of the story, and He is the only one qualified to
judge people for what they've done.

*God, I know how much You love me, and I know
You've seen everything that has happened. When I'm
tempted to give in to my anger and pay someone back
for their wrongs, please remind me that You are in control.
Help me to trust You more.*

Being Generous

*Tell those rich in this world's wealth to quit being so full
of themselves and so obsessed with money, which is here
today and gone tomorrow. Tell them to go after God,
who piles on all the riches we could ever manage—to do good,
to be rich in helping others, to be extravagantly generous.
If they do that, they'll build a treasury that will last,
gaining life that is truly life.*

1 TIMOTHY 6:18–19 MSG

This verse in The Message translation of the Bible really
tells it like it is! Having lots of money and getting more
money is the number one priority on many people's list.
What about yours? Do you find yourself wishing you had
a lot more money than you do? Do you keep wishing for
more and more stuff? Ask God to change your desires to
match His. Ask Him to make you extra generous with what
you already have and to have a giving heart. God wants us
to run after Him. . .not money and things that don't last.

*God, forgive me for the times I can only think about getting
more. I don't want to live like that. Help me be content with
what I have, and please give me a generous heart.*

Forgiveness

Do not hold against us the sins of past generations;
may your mercy come quickly to meet us, for we are in
desperate need. Help us, God our Savior, for the glory of your
name; deliver us and forgive our sins for your name's sake.
PSALM 79:8–9 NIV

Nineteenth-century poet, writer, and playwright Oscar Wilde said "After a good dinner one can forgive anybody, even one's own relatives." Family and forgiveness go hand in hand. Families are made up of a bunch of imperfect people. Some are trying to follow the Lord and some are very far from God. God calls us to love them all—and to forgive. Max Lucado said, "Forgiveness is unlocking the door to set someone free and realizing you were the prisoner!" Forgiveness is not about sweeping things under the rug and pretending. Forgiveness is bold. It is facing the facts about people and their sinful nature, and choosing to love and forgive in spite of hurt and hard feelings. Don't be a prisoner because you're refusing to forgive. Let go and allow God to change your heart and set you free.

God, please help me to forgive others
as You have forgiven me.

Share What You Have

*Do not neglect to do good and to share what you have,
for such sacrifices are pleasing to God.*
HEBREWS 13:16 ESV

You may have a little. . .or you may have a lot. Whatever you've been given, God wants you to have a generous heart. Even if you don't have much to share, you can bless someone with whatever you do have. Be willing to share. This means more than just being willing to share your things. God has blessed you with special gifts and talents that only you have. God wants to use you to bless others with those gifts He's given you. If you can't give extravagant gifts, make something from your heart. Homemade gifts or services mean a lot more to people in the long run, anyway. . .especially when it's for someone in your family. Grandmas and Grandpa love getting homemade gifts. Moms and Dads treasure the things you make for them. Who wouldn't love to have a special dessert made by you or a chore done for them? There are lots and lots of things you can share, even if you don't have a penny!

*God, thanks for the gifts You've given me. Show me ways
that I can share them with others.*

Commit Yourself to God

*So then, those who suffer according to God's will
should commit themselves to their faithful Creator
and continue to do good.*

1 PETER 4:19 NIV

Sometimes bad things happen to good people. Jesus reminds us often that we live in a broken world, full of broken people that do broken things. Because He gave us all the freedom to choose, our actions and reactions are based on those choices. Sometimes we do suffer for the choices we make: the good and the bad. Take heart! There is no reason to be afraid because God has already won the battle. His Spirit who is alive in you can give you the power to overcome any suffering with joy in your heart. So during the precious time you've been given on this earth, commit yourself to your faithful Creator. He is over all and in all and through all (see Ephesians 4:6), and He holds all things together (see Colossians 1:17). Keep doing what God wants you to do, and remember that He loves you desperately! He is always with you.

*God, I commit my whole heart to You. It's hard when bad
things happen, but I know You're always with me.*

Hungry and Thirsty

*"Blessed are those who hunger and thirst for righteousness,
for they shall be satisfied."*
MATTHEW 5:6 ESV

. . . .

Have you ever been so thirsty you could hardly stand it?
Or have you ever been so hungry your stomach started to
growl in the middle of class? Jesus wants us to hunger and
thirst after Him just like we would for food or drink. One
day Jesus was talking to a woman who was getting water
out of a well. He said: "Everyone who drinks of this water
will be thirsty again, but whoever drinks of the water that
I will give him will never be thirsty again. The water that I
will give him will become in him a spring of water welling
up to eternal life" (John 4:13-14 ESV). When we thirst after
God and His righteousness, He fills us up with living water
like a spring that bubbles up and over bringing life to everything around it. Be hungry and thirsty for God and you
will be full of His life and love forever!

*God, I know I'll be hungry and thirsty for food and drink
today. When I am, please remind me that I need to be filled
up with Your love first—that's the most important thing of all!*

Seeking God

But seek first the kingdom of God and his righteousness,
and all these things will be added to you.
MATTHEW 6:33 ESV

In Matthew 6:25–34, Jesus is telling His followers not to worry. Just like we do today, people were worrying about what to wear and what to eat. He reminds us of the birds and the flowers. They don't go around worrying because God has made provision for them. Birds find food, and flowers are created to be beautiful. God says not to worry because He knows that we need to have clothes and that we need to eat. He promises to provide for our needs. You might not be dressed in designer jeans or eat like a king every day, but when you seek God's kingdom first. . .He'll make sure you have exactly what you need. God wants us to come to Him and passionately seek Him in all things. He delights in meeting your needs and blessing you. Keep watch for the blessings God sends as you follow Him. . . they are all around you!

God, help me not to miss the blessings You have for me
each and every day. Help me to be on the lookout as
You show up in big and small ways as I seek You.

Get Rid of the Gossip

The mouths of fools are their undoing, and their lips are a snare to their very lives. The words of a gossip are like choice morsels; they go down to the inmost parts.

PROVERBS 18:7–8 NIV

People often make light of gossip and even encourage it under the guise of "just wanting to help." Yet we all know that gossip hurts. No one likes to walk into a room only to hear "the hush" and realize they were the topic of discussion. This happens so many times in friendships. The truth is, it is easy to participate in gossip. It can sneak up on you when you are least expecting it. It's been said that if you have to glance at the door to see if anyone is coming before you begin a conversation with someone, you probably shouldn't be having that conversation! Gossip is no laughing matter. God takes it very seriously. It hurts others, it ruins friendship, and it is never harmless.

God, please forgive me for the times I've gossiped about other people. I know gossip is hurtful, and I'm sorry. Please help me to watch my words.

Build Others Up

*Do not let any unwholesome talk come out of your mouths,
but only what is helpful for building others up according to
their needs, that it may benefit those who listen.*

EPHESIANS 4:29 NIV

Words are powerful. They can build people up or they can
tear them down. Have you been affected by other people's
words? Have you ever had someone you respect say really
nice things about you? It feels good, right? It makes you
feel like you have value as a person. Have you ever had
someone say some really bad things about you? If so, you
know how much it hurts. Every time you speak to someone
you can leave them feeling better or worse about themselves. You can encourage them and help them feel like
they can accomplish more in their life or you can discour-
age them and leave them with negative thoughts. Pray for
God to help you speak words that encourage people.

*God, please help me to build other people up and
encourage them with my words. I want to leave them
feeling encouraged and hopeful. Show me how to
speak the truth in loving ways.*

Good Conversation

Let your conversation be always full of grace, seasoned with salt, so that you may know how to answer everyone.

COLOSSIANS 4:6 NIV

It's always so sad to hear of Christians fighting with other Christians. Yes, we absolutely must stand up for truth and defend truth passionately. However, there is a right way and wrong way to do it. God wants us to speak truth in love (see Ephesians 4:15), and He wants everything about our lives to be marked by His love. . .especially our conversations! Over and over in the Bible, God talks to us about our words:

Be quick to listen and slow to speak (see James 1:19).

People will give an account for every careless word they speak (see Matthew 12:36).

Those who consider themselves religious and yet do not keep a tight rein on their tongues deceive themselves, and their religion is worthless (see James 1:26).

These are just a few! Our words are so important, and once they're said out loud. . .you can't take them back. Ask God to help you with your words!

God, please help me to bring all of my words to You first, before I say them to someone else. I want to honor You with my words and bring hope and love to people by them.

Keeping a Confidence

It is foolish to belittle one's neighbor; a sensible person keeps quiet. A gossip goes around telling secrets, but those who are trustworthy can keep a confidence.
PROVERBS 11:12–13 NLT

Are you trustworthy? That's what keeping a confidence is all about. Your friends want to know that they can trust you. Do you have any friends or family members that talk about others as soon as they leave the room? Those people are not trustworthy because you know that they'll talk about you when you leave the room, too. Don't be fooled into thinking that they won't do that to you just because they say you are their friend. The Bible says that sensible and trustworthy people don't act like that. People who love God want the best for you and they won't put you down when you aren't around. Think about what kind of person you are: Do your friends trust you? Should they?

God, please help me to love You and love others well. Help me to be trustworthy, and forgive me for the times I haven't been. Help me to find trustworthy friends that love You and want to please You with their lives.

Undeserved Kindness

We are made right with God by placing our faith in Jesus Christ. And this is true for everyone who believes, no matter who we are. For everyone has sinned; we all fall short of God's glorious standard. Yet God freely and graciously declares that we are righteous. He did this through Christ Jesus when he freed us from the penalty for our sins.

ROMANS 3:22–24 NLT

. . . .

Take some time to re-read that verse several times over. Let it sink in. Ask God to give you wisdom as you read those words and trust that they are true. In God's great and undeserved kindness, He has declared us righteous— completely clean in the blood of Christ! He took all of our sin and shame on Himself and set us free. We are right with God! If you have a journal, write down how that makes you feel inside. When someone gives us a special gift, we write them a thank you note, right? Spend a few minutes writing God a thank you note for His great gift.

God, Your kindness makes my heart glad. I don't understand how You did something like this, but I'm truly thankful. Please help me never to take the death of Your Son for granted. I want to live for You, God!

Keeping the Faith

*And if God cares so wonderfully for wildflowers that are
here today and thrown into the fire tomorrow, he will
certainly care for you. Why do you have so little faith?*
MATTHEW 6:30 NLT

Our enemy loves to distract us and get us to worry. When
we worry, our focus is never on Christ. . .so the enemy wins!
Stress and worry and anxiety are all signs that we don't
trust God very much. It means that God is very small in
our life and our faith is small. So what can be done about
that? Go to God and confess your lack of faith. When people and things are big in our life. . .God doesn't have the
room He needs to be big in your world. That means there
are idols in your heart. Anything that comes between you
and God—whether it's good or bad—is an idol. Maybe it is
someone you love and their opinion of you matters more
than God. Or maybe your desire for something is so great
that it is getting in the way of what God wants to do in
your life. Lay all of these at the feet of Jesus and allow Him
to increase your faith.

*God, please remove any idols in my heart.
I want You to be big in my life!*

God Made the Box

*You hem me in behind and before, and you lay
your hand upon me. Such knowledge is too
wonderful for me, too lofty for me to attain.*

PSALM 139:5-6 NIV

How is it possible for God to care about my thoughts and
feelings? With billions of people to watch over, how can
he possibly know me? When we limit our thinking to what
we believe to be possible, we put God in a box. God is the
Divine Creator. He made the box. The Bible says that such
knowledge is too much for us to grasp. God is the God of
the impossible (see Luke 1:37). He is beyond the limitations
of the human mind. The truth is: He *does* know you. He
does care. He loves you beyond what your mind can fully
understand. He just does. It's a faith thing. Ephesians 3:20
tells us that God is able to do exceedingly, abundantly
more than what we could ever ask or even think! Caring
about us personally is one of those things.

*God, please open up my heart and strengthen my faith in
You. Help me to believe even more than I already do.*

In All Your Ways

*Trust in the LORD with all your heart and lean not
on your own understanding; in all your ways submit
to him, and he will make your paths straight.*
PROVERBS 3:5-6 NIV

How many times do we set out to do something that was
never ours to do? We try to fix a problem that isn't ours
to fix. We try to help a situation that we're not meant to
help. We often get mixed up in things that we shouldn't.
God wants us to acknowledge and come to Him before
and during our plans. Does this mean if you've made a bad
choice and taken a wrong path that you're on your own?
Absolutely not. God has promised to never leave you!
Trust Him to help you get back on the path that was meant
for you. Yeah, it might be a little messy trying to get out of
a situation you've put yourself in! Yet God is faithful even
when we make a mess of things. Once you begin to trust
the Lord with all of your heart, you'll begin to seek Him
first and trust that He will guide you.

*God, please help me to get back on the right path. I want to
trust You with all of my heart and come to You first.*

Nothing Is Impossible

"I tell you the truth, if you had faith even as small as a mustard seed, you could say to this mountain, 'Move from here to there,' and it would move. Nothing would be impossible."
MATTHEW 17:20 NLT

Have you ever seen a mustard seed? Look for a jar of them the next time you're at the grocery store. They are very tiny! God tells us that even if we have faith *that* small—He will show up in *big* ways! It's not about the size of our faith—it's about the power of God. God doesn't want us to trust in ourselves and in our own faith. Faith is all about putting our trust in the Living God and knowing that when we are weak, He is strong! It's about taking our eyes off of the problems and praying for God to show up and do His thing. When you are facing mountains in your life, think about the mustard seed. Ask God to remind you that He is much bigger than your mountain!

God, my faith is small like a mustard seed. I pray You would increase my faith in You. . .not in what I can do. Remind me that You are great and I am small. . . yet still You love and care for me always.

Ask for Faithfulness

*"The master was full of praise. 'Well done, my good
and faithful servant. You have been faithful in handling
this small amount, so now I will give you many more
responsibilities. Let's celebrate together!' "*

MATTHEW 25:21 NLT

God has given us all work to do on this earth as we wait
for Him to come back. He's given each of us gifts and
talents to use to serve Him and share His love with others
while we have the time. We want God to tell us we've done
a good job doing His work here. Then, when we've been
faithful in doing certain tasks for God, He'll give us more
and more tasks to finish. Mother Teresa once said: "I do not
pray for success; I ask for faithfulness." She may have said
that because humans easily lose interest in a job once they
are stuck on a problem or bored with it. Finishing the job
requires lots and lots of faithfulness. Finishing the job well
requires lots of prayer and dependence on God.

*God, I ask that You would help me to be faithful in all
the tasks that You give me on this earth. Help me not
to lose hope when problems come but to finish the job
well as I trust in You for help.*

Faithful in Much

"One who is faithful in a very little is also faithful in much, and one who is dishonest in a very little is also dishonest in much."

LUKE 16:10 ESV

If you asked your friend to feed your fish while you went away on vacation and you came home to find your fish happy and well-fed, you just might be willing to let that same friend watch your hamster, too. Then maybe even your dog, right? That's kind of like what Jesus is saying in this verse. If someone is faithful in the little things, they'll also be faithful in the big things. However, if your friend forgot to feed your fish for a day or two, she'd probably forget to feed your dog, too. Even if she begged you to let her keep your dog for a week, you probably wouldn't, because actions speak louder than words. If she wasn't trustworthy with something small. . .she won't be trustworthy with something big. It's the same with us, of course. If God gives you something small to do and you do it well. . . He will trust you to do even greater things.

God, I want to be faithful to You in all things—big and small. Help me to be a trustworthy person.

Faithful in All Things

And if you are not faithful with other people's things,
why should you be trusted with things of your own?
LUKE 16:12 NLT

. . . .

Have you ever borrowed clothes from a friend? Maybe she
let you borrow her best outfit for something special. Would
you run out to the park in the rain with that outfit on. . .or
decide to paint a masterpiece while wearing it? Of course
not! Because you know how special that outfit is to your
friend. You wear it carefully and lovingly. Jesus wants us to
respect other people and the things that are important to
them. When you borrow a book from a library, you have to
treat it well or the librarian will give you a fine. When you
prove trustworthy with other people's things, they'll want
to trust you with more and more. Remember the golden
rule: treat each other as you would like to be treated. That
also applies to things. Treat other people's things the way
you'd want them to treat your things!

Thank You, God, for friends who trust me. Help me to
be faithful and respectful of other people and the things
that are important to them.

My Times Are in Your Hands

But I trust in you, LORD; I say, "You are my God."
My times are in your hands; deliver me from the hands
of my enemies, from those who pursue me.

PSALM 31:14–15 NIV

Day-to-day trusting God keeps you from being sucked into the constant craziness of life, where crisis surrounds and drama abounds. Trusting God makes our problems seem so much smaller when we think about heaven and all that God has planned for those who love Him. While life may be hard and confusing at times, we know that all of our times are in God's hands. He sees it all and Has a miraculous plan to make everything right! So when trouble comes knocking at your door—and it will—you don't have to freak out! You can say, "I trust in You, Lord! My times are in Your hands. I know You've got this. I trust Your faithfulness. This looks hard, but I know it'll be okay."

God, help me to trust You day by day and moment
by moment. I feel a lot of pressure sometimes to make big
decisions about my future, but I know
You hold it all in Your hands.

God Is Present

How abundant are the good things that you have stored up for those who fear you, that you bestow in the sight of all, on those who take refuge in you.

PSALM 31:19 NIV

When you trust God, He becomes your refuge; A very present help in times of trouble (see Psalm 46:1)! A *very present* help. Think about that for a minute: God is very present. . . . He is with you this very moment as you read these words. His power and comfort are constantly available to you. He is good, and He wants to show His goodness to you on a daily basis. When you focus on all the bad things and worry about stuff that hasn't even happened yet, you forget about God. However, when you focus on God and talk to Him instead of worrying, He actually shows Himself to you in each moment. We may live in a broken world—but we have great *hope*! Because He is with us. . .our times are in His hands. . .and His perfect plan is trustworthy!

God, thank You again and again for being with me in each moment. Forgive me for the times I worry. Please replace my worries with Your peace.

Jesus among Us

So the Word became human and made his home among us.
He was full of unfailing love and faithfulness. And we have
seen his glory, the glory of the Father's one and only Son.
JOHN 1:14 NLT

. . . .

God is God, and He could have chosen a million different
ways to save us, but He chose to show us the true meaning
of love. Greater love has no one than this: to lay down one's
life for one's friends (see John 15:13). Giving up your life
for someone else is true, unselfish love. God chose to send
His Son into the world to live just like us, to become our
friend. . .and to eventually lay down His life and die on the
cross to show how much He actually loves us. Jesus knew
it would hurt. He knew He would suffer. He knew He would
be betrayed by some of the people closest to Him. Yet He
did it all anyway so that we could be made right with God—
once and for all. His unfailing love is available to all of us
who seek Him!

God, Your unfailing love for me is something I'll always be
trying to figure out. Thank You for sending Jesus
to make me right with You. I love You, Lord!

Remain Faithful

Jesus said to the people who believed in him, "You are truly my disciples if you remain faithful to my teachings."
JOHN 8:31 NLT

. . . .

Have you ever read through Matthew, Mark, Luke, and John? These books of the Bible are called "The Gospels" and they teach us about the life and words of Jesus. If you've never read much of the Bible, these books are some of the best books to start with. You can learn how Jesus came into the world, how He lived, and the words He said. He didn't just say them to His twelve disciples, way back two thousand years ago. . . His words are meant for you today, too. Jesus said that if we really want to follow Him we need to be faithful to His teachings. That means we need to get into His word and find out what He says. If you don't own a Bible, you can usually get one for free at church. . . and you can even download a free Bible app online! Jesus' teachings have stood the test of time, and He has a lot to say to you, too!

God, I want to be a faithful follower of You. Please put the desire in my heart to know Your words and to learn more about what Jesus has to say to me.

Walking with God

For you have rescued me from death; you have kept
my feet from slipping. So now I can walk in your
presence, O God, in your life-giving light.

PSALM 56:13 NLT

A moment-by-moment relationship with God gives us an eternal perspective. Walking with God is not just reading a Bible verse each morning and checking God off your list for the day. It is not being a regular member at church serving in whatever way is needed. . .and leaving faith in the box until the next Sunday. It is a daily walk with God. It is a moment-by-moment conversation with Christ. First Thessalonians 5:16–18 says: "Rejoice always, pray continually, give thanks in all circumstances; for this is God's will for you in Christ Jesus." Walking with God is having a relationship with your Creator. It is knowing Him, loving Him, trusting Him, and worshipping Him in each moment. The Bible promises that we can walk in His presence each and every moment! What does that look like? It's inviting God into every conversation you have, every thought you think, and everything you do.

God, help me to be constantly aware of Your Presence
in my life. I want to know You more.

Just Believe!

*Then he said to Thomas, "Put your finger here,
and look at my hands. Put your hand into the wound
in my side. Don't be faithless any longer. Believe!"*
JOHN 20:27 NLT

Thomas was one of Jesus' original twelve disciples. He
was with Jesus during His ministry on earth and yet
still had a hard time believing that Jesus rose from the
dead. Even after witnessing the many miracles of Jesus
firsthand! Jesus knew that Thomas needed to see His
scars for Him to believe so He showed them to Thomas
up close. When Jesus allowed Thomas to touch Him
He said: "Have you believed because you have seen
me? Blessed are those who have not seen and yet have
believed" (John 20:29). Sometimes we wish we could see
Jesus face-to-face just like Thomas. Did you catch what
Jesus said to Thomas? "Blessed are those who have not
seen and yet have believed." Jesus was talking about you
and me! He said we are blessed because we have faith
without actually seeing Him with our own eyes.

*God, help me believe even though I can't see. Increase my
faith in You, and help me to hear You speak to me through
Your Word. Thank You for blessing me!*

Seek and Trust

*But the LORD sits enthroned forever; he has established his
throne for justice, and he judges the world with
righteousness; he judges the peoples with uprightness.
The LORD is a stronghold for the oppressed, a stronghold
in times of trouble. And those who know your name
put their trust in you, for you, O LORD,
have not forsaken those who seek you.*

PSALM 9:7–10 ESV

When you walk with God, you experience His absolute
faithfulness. This brings trust—a deep knowing—that God
is ultimately good and has your best interests in mind.
Things will happen along the way which don't make any
sense to us at the time. We experience pain and sadness
that comes with living in a messed-up world. As we seek
God, we begin to see purpose in our troubles. He turns
everything around for our good and His glory! God has
purpose in everything. He is just. He is righteous, and He
is good.

*God, I trust that You will never forsake me—You'll never
let me down! You are my stronghold—my fortress and my
refuge. I know I can come to You and find shelter and safety
in Your arms. Help me to seek You and trust
You always with all of my heart.*

Confident and Joyful

Because of our faith, Christ has brought us into this place of undeserved privilege where we now stand, and we confidently and joyfully look forward to sharing God's glory.

ROMANS 5:2 NLT

Because of all that Jesus did for us on the cross, He made us children of God! However, we're not just His children, now. . .He actually calls us His friend (see John 15:13–15)! Have you ever thought about what being a friend of God means? When you look for a friend you want someone who is kind, trustworthy, and willing to listen. God wants to have that very same kind of relationship with you. He wants you to know that you are never, *ever* alone! He wants you to live a life of confidence and joy, knowing that God is working everything out for your good and His glory—even the bad things that happen during this life. When trouble comes your way, you can look at it with peace knowing that your very best friend has it covered.

God, how awesome that You call me Your friend! That makes me confident that I can go through life with joy in my heart!

Be Yourself

*Everything God created is good, and to be received with
thanks. Nothing is to be sneered at and thrown out. God's
Word and our prayers make every item in creation holy.*

1 TIMOTHY 4:4–5 MSG

God created you, and everything He created is good! So
just be the person God created you to be. You might wish
your personality was just like someone else's or that you
had different hair or skin. . .but God created you exactly
the way He wanted you. Your personality is the way God
made you, and He wants to use that for His glory. He gave
you the body you have for a reason. . .so take good care
of it and thank Him for it. Ask God to change your heart
to match His desire for you. God looks at You and sees
His beautiful work of art. Ask Him to give you that same
attitude about yourself—not so you'll be full of yourself, but
so you will respect and enjoy the body and personality God
gave you!

*God, please change my heart to match Yours.
Sometimes it's hard for me to see myself as beautiful.
Help me to know that it is true. Help me to be myself—
just the way You made me.*

Gentle and Kindhearted

A kindhearted woman gains honor,
but ruthless men gain only wealth.
PROVERBS 11:16 NIV

The Message version of this verse says "a woman of gentle grace gets respect." A gentle and kindhearted woman earns the respect of other people. . .and they listen to her and go to her for advice. An obnoxious woman is avoided and is not trustworthy. No matter what kind of personality you have—outgoing, quiet, very sensitive or more logical. . . maybe you're musical and artistic, or maybe you love to lead and like to get things done—God gave you that personality for a purpose. He wants you to bring your whole self to Him so that He can make you into the woman He wants you to be. He wants to fill you with the fruit of His Spirit which include gentleness and self-control. He wants His children to respect others and for people to respect them in return. Ask God to help keep your focus on Him and to use your personality for His glory!

God, thank You for the personality You gave me!
I know I am the way I am for a purpose. Please show me
how to be more gentle and kindhearted.

Gentle Answers

*A gentle answer turns away wrath,
but a harsh word stirs up anger.*
PROVERBS 15:1 NIV

. . . .

Do you know anyone who loves to argue? Maybe you've
seen someone on TV who always wants to get his or her
own way and they argue with anyone who says differently.
When one person is yelling at another, it stirs up anger in
the other person. Then the arguing gets louder and louder
and angrier and angrier. Yet if you answer someone with
gentleness, it can turn off their anger. If it doesn't. . .you
can just walk away. Proverbs 29:11 (NRSV) says "A fool gives
full vent to anger, but the wise quietly holds it back." You
know that anyone with a hot temper who spews whatever
comes to their mind is a fool. If you're wise, you'll take your
thoughts to God first before sharing them with someone
else. Saint Francis de Sales said "Nothing is so strong as
gentleness, nothing so gentle as real strength."

*God, help me to be strong and gentle at the same time.
Please give me Your strength as I face anyone who may
be angry in the future. Help me to answer
gently or to walk away.*

Tree of Life

Gentle words are a tree of life;
a deceitful tongue crushes the spirit.
PROVERBS 15:4 NLT

. . . .

Have you ever been lied to? Maybe a friend or family member that you trust told you something that is not true on purpose. Hopefully that hasn't happened to you, but if it has, you know that it feels like you've been punched in the gut. The Bible tells us that a liar crushes other people's spirits. However, gentle words that are true can be healing and life-giving. Remember, words are very powerful! Once said, you can never really take them back. . .even if you want to. You can use words for good or for evil. Eighteenth-century writer William Hazlitt said: "A gentle word, a kind look, a good-natured smile can work wonders and accomplish miracles." Do you think that is true? Why not give it a try today. Go out of your way to bring kind words to people you usually don't talk to. Greet people with a smile and an encouraging word. Ask God to use your words to bring people life today.

God, please help me to be very careful with my words. Help
me to encourage others and bring them a smile and kind
words. Use my words to bring other people to You.

Be Wise

There's nothing better than being wise, Knowing how to interpret the meaning of life. Wisdom puts light in the eyes, And gives gentleness to words and manners.

ECCLESIASTES 8:1 MSG

When King Solomon was made king, God appeared to Him in a dream and told Solomon to ask for whatever He wanted. Instead of asking for riches or selfish things, Solomon asked God for wisdom. God was pleased by this and said, "I will give you what you asked for! I will give you a wise and understanding heart such as no one else has had or ever will have" (1 Kings 3:12 NLT). Solomon's request for wisdom made God happy, and He made him the wisest man that ever lived. However, if you read about Solomon's life, he ended up making a lot of poor decisions. Being wise isn't just about knowing all the right answers, it's about putting them into practice. Solomon was a wise ruler, but he didn't apply his wisdom to his personal life and that got him into a lot of trouble.

God, I pray that You would give me wisdom to know Your will—and to do it, too. Help me to make wise decisions that please You.

Nobody's Perfect

*Always be humble and gentle. Be patient
with each other, making allowance for each
other's faults because of your love.*

EPHESIANS 4:2 NLT

You can probably think of at least two or three people
that really annoy you. Have you ever thought about why
they act the way they do? Maybe they aren't getting their
needs met from their parents and they are trying to get
attention and affection from anyone else they can. There
is always a reason for why people act the way they do, even
if they don't know it themselves. God knows! That's why
you should pray for the people that bother you. God knows
exactly why they act the way they do, and your prayers can
help change that person's heart—and yours in the process!
Nobody's perfect and even your best friend will act in ways
that bother you at some time or another. Make allowance
for that because of God's love living inside you. Be patient
and gentle with others.

*God, I don't understand why people act the way they do,
but I pray You would help me love them anyway.
The next time I'm extremely annoyed at someone,
please remind me to pray for them!*

A Clean Break

Make a clean break with all cutting, backbiting,
profane talk. Be gentle with one another, sensitive.
Forgive one another as quickly and thoroughly
as God in Christ forgave you.
EPHESIANS 4:31 MSG

Have you been known to say some words that might not please God? Maybe you get easily annoyed at your brother or sister and you lash out at them easily? Ask God to help you make a clean break! Ask Him to allow you to stop saying and doing those things cold turkey! God wants to help you become more like Him, and He is able to work miracles in your life today. He can help you to stop being harsh with others and replace that with gentleness and forgiveness. The next time you find yourself ready to lash out at someone. . .stop right in your tracks. Quiet your heart before God, and ask Him to keep your words gentle and sensitive. Then walk away if you need to and come back when you are calmer! Sometimes walking away is the most loving thing you can do in the moment.

God, please give me a clean break from harsh words
and actions that I've been known to do. Help me, God.
Give me wisdom in this area.

Evidence of Gentleness

Let your gentleness be evident to all. The Lord is near.
PHILIPPIANS 4:5 NIV

Do people know you as a gentle person? Even if your personality is more outgoing and silly. . .are you gentle when it comes to more serious matters? Remember, God made your personality and He loves you just the way you are. He doesn't want to change the personality He gave you. He just wants you to bring your whole self to Him and let Him work in your life to make you all that He desires for you to be. God wants to use you in great ways! He can do that when you humble yourself and come before Him, asking for a clean and pure heart. . .full of love and gentleness. God is always near. The Bible tells us that Jesus could come back at any moment so His coming is near. His Spirit is always with you, too. Even now. Ask Him to cultivate gentleness in your heart so that all who know you will see evidence of God in your life.

God, I want there to be evidence of gentleness that points to You in my life. Thank You for always being near me. Help me to constantly reach out for You.

God's Kind of Clothes

*Therefore, as God's chosen people, holy and dearly loved,
clothe yourselves with compassion, kindness, humility,
gentleness and patience.*

COLOSSIANS 3:12 NIV

A girl can't leave the house without the basics, right? Her
favorite jeans, cute shoes, matching nail polish. Wait! God
says there are even more important things for us to "wear"
each day. He wants us to put on compassion, kindness,
humility, gentleness, and patience. Our new basics need to
be based on love. Love for God and love for others. That's
what really matters! God loves you dearly, and you already
know that. He loves everyone else, too, and some of them
might not know it yet. He wants you to share His love with
others. He wants you to be kind and truly care for others
and to love like Jesus loves. Next time you're headed out,
reach for God's kind of clothes, and you'll be ready for
anything.

*God, I know how much You love me! You fill me up with
it every single day. Help me share that love with everyone
I meet. Help me to wear things that matter for eternity:
love, compassion, kindness, and all of
the qualities that please You.*

Be Gentle

*Remind the people to be subject to rulers and authorities,
to be obedient, to be ready to do whatever is good,
to slander no one, to be peaceable and considerate,
and always to be gentle toward everyone.*

TITUS 3:1–2 NIV

The Bible talks quite a bit about being gentle. It's something we often overlook in today's world. Even in the church, people get extra busy and distracted and gentleness isn't a focus. Often, we say whatever we feel whether it hurts somebody else's feelings or not. God doesn't want us to live this way. He wants us to be gentle with each other. Just like new parents are gentle with their newborn baby; we need to be gentle in our words and actions toward others. If you have something important to say, say it! Say it with gentleness and love in your heart. We talk a lot about being "real" or "authentic" today. Yet that doesn't give us an excuse to blurt out whatever we feel like saying without caring about other people's feelings. Take all your words and actions to God first, and He will help you respond in gentleness and love.

*God, I want to be real with You and others, but please help
me to do that gently and with love in my heart.*

Precious to God

Don't be concerned about the outward beauty of fancy hairstyles, expensive jewelry, or beautiful clothes. You should clothe yourselves instead with the beauty that comes from within, the unfading beauty of a gentle and quiet spirit, which is so precious to God.

1 PETER 3:3–4 NLT

Do you ever wish you were created with different hair or a prettier face? God wants you to know that you are beautiful just the way you are! Besides, what you think is pretty now will change in a few years. Did you know that fat women were considered the most beautiful of all in other cultures? Pale white skin used to be a sign of beauty and royalty. Just because our culture prizes certain women for looking thin and tan today doesn't mean that will last. It means nothing to God! God sees you from the inside. He wants your beauty to shine from a clean heart. You don't need the best hair or designer clothes to be precious to God. You are His princess, and He created you just the way you are.

God, please make my heart beautiful and pure. I want to follow You, and I want my beauty to shine from inside. Thanks for creating me just the way I am.

Gentleness and Respect

*But in your hearts revere Christ as Lord. Always be
prepared to give an answer to everyone who asks you to give
the reason for the hope that you have. But do this with
gentleness and respect, keeping a clear conscience,
so that those who speak maliciously against your good
behavior in Christ may be ashamed of their slander.*

1 PETER 3:15–16 NIV

If you're living your life to follow Christ, other people
are going to wonder about you! If you love God and treat
other people with kindness, you're going to get questions
about why you do what you do. Are you ready to answer
them? Some people may be unkind and make fun of you
for being a Christian. Their words might make you angry.
Before you answer them, ask for God's help. He is right
there with you, and He sees everything that's happening.
He wants you to answer with gentleness and respect, not
anger and embarrassment. The reason they're asking
is because they are looking for hope, too! They want to
know if yours is real or not!

*God, help me remember that everyone else is looking for
hope in You, too. You created them that way. Help me be
gentle and respect others when I share my faith in You.*

In the Garden

You will always harvest what you plant. Those who live only to satisfy their own sinful nature will harvest decay and death from that sinful nature. But those who live to please the Spirit will harvest everlasting life from the Spirit.

GALATIANS 6:7-8 NLT

Do you like to grow things? In school, you've probably learned about planting seeds and watching them grow. Jesus liked to use gardening illustrations in the Bible to help people understand what he was teaching, too! John chapter 15 is another good example of this. Jesus says: "Yes, I am the vine; you are the branches. Those who remain in me, and I in them, will produce much fruit" (verse 5 NLT). You can learn a lot by hanging out in the garden. Yet, even if you're not a big fan of digging in the dirt, just appreciate all the beautiful flowers and plants that God created. When you see them, view them as reminders that God wants to fill you up with the fruit of His Spirit.

God, thank You for the many different kinds of plants and flowers I see in Your creation. Use them to remind me of Your teachings, to guide me to do the right thing, and to help me grow into the kind of woman You want me to be.

Filled with Fruit

*I pray that your love will overflow more and more,
and that you will keep on growing in knowledge and
understanding. For I want you to understand what really
matters, so that you may live pure and blameless lives until
the day of Christ's return. May you always be filled with the
fruit of your salvation—the righteous character produced in
your life by Jesus Christ—for this will bring much
glory and praise to God.*

PHILIPPIANS 1:9–11 NLT

The fruit of the Spirit is a really big deal! When the Spirit
of God is at work in your heart, He produces fruit because
of Jesus' work on the cross. Check out Galatians 5:22–23
again! Do you have fruit growing in your life right now?
Can you see love, joy, peace, patience, kindness, goodness,
gentleness, faithfulness, and self-control taking root and
expanding in your heart? If you can, this brings much
glory to God! If you're not sure, start talking to God about
it. Ask Him to clear out your heart to make room for what
He wants to plant there.

*God, please fill me up with the fruit of Your Spirit.
I want to see You at work in my life.*

Set an Example

*Don't let anyone look down on you because you
are young, but set an example for the believers
in speech, in conduct, in love, in faith and in purity.*
1 TIMOTHY 4:12 NIV

When you've committed your life to Christ, His Spirit
comes and lives inside of you—and He gives you the power
to be an example to others. . .even older generations. Sometimes it takes the faith of a child to get a hardened heart
to hear God's Word. You never know when your life will
touch someone else, but you can be sure that everyone you
know is watching to see if your faith is making a difference
in your life. There was a Native American leader named
Tecumseh who said: "Show respect to all people, but grovel
to none." That is another way of saying "don't let anyone
look down on you." Even if there are adults in your life who
try their hardest to put you down, you are a child of God
and He is the one who determines your value. Never forget
that!

*God, thank You for showing me who I am in You!
Help me to be a good example to others!*

Pure, Holy, and Free!

*God has united you with Christ Jesus. For our benefit God
made him to be wisdom itself. Christ made us right with
God; he made us pure and holy, and he freed us from sin.*

1 CORINTHIANS 1:30 NLT

The Bible tells us that the wages of sin is death (see
Romans 6:23), but the gift of God is eternal life! God is
holy, and holiness cannot live where sin lives. Since we're
human and we have all chosen to sin, God sent Jesus to
take our payment. He died to make us right with God for
the sins we've already committed and any sin we'll commit
in the future. Does that mean we should keep on sinning
and not worry about it? No way! That would be taking the
death of Jesus and the pain He endured for you for granted.
He bled and hung on a cross for you with nails piercing
His skin so that you could be with God forever. When God
looks at us, He sees us as pure, holy, and free because of
what Jesus did for us on the cross.

*God, I never want to take Jesus' death for granted.
I'm so thankful that You love me so much.
Help me to live pure, holy, and free!*

Shining Like a Star

Do everything without grumbling or arguing, so that you
may become blameless and pure, "children of God
without fault in a warped and crooked generation."
Then you will shine among them like stars in the sky
as you hold firmly to the word of life.

PHILIPPIANS 2:14–16 NIV

Seems like everyone wants to be a superstar these days, right? Even young teens make music videos on YouTube and they become famous instantly. What's the big deal about being a star? Sure, you get lots and lots of attention, make lots of money, and buy whatever you want. Just take a look at the lives of people who were stars at a young age. Most of them grow up and make a mess of their lives, and many even die young because they were seeking love in all the wrong places. You are a child of God, and you are loved desperately! God gives you all the attention you could ever want, and His desire is for you to shine for Him. If you live like that, you'll stand out for sure!

God, help me live a different kind of life than everyone else.
The world seeks things that don't matter. I want to seek You.
Help me light up the world with Your love!

Whatcha Thinkin' About?

Finally, brothers and sisters, whatever is true, whatever is noble, whatever is right, whatever is pure, whatever is lovely, whatever is admirable—if anything is excellent or praiseworthy—think about such things.

PHILIPPIANS 4:8 NIV

Our thoughts can get us in lots and lots of trouble. It's easy to get off track and think about things we shouldn't. . .even when we're praying! We start off thinking about something good. . .then we remember something else. . .then our thoughts jump to something else and something else and something else, and before we know it, we've stopped praying and we're thinking about something entirely different than what we started praying about! The next time you find yourself thinking about something that isn't right, ask God to step right into your thoughts and change them! Just speak His name and ask Him to come to your rescue. He can change the direction of your thoughts and turn them into thoughts and actions that are pure and true and lovely. The name of Jesus has power in heaven and earth (see Philippians 2:10), and just speaking His name will change things. . .even your thoughts!

Jesus, Your name is power. I pray You will step in and change my thoughts to be pure and true!

Don't Conform. . .Transform!

*And so, dear brothers and sisters, I plead with you to give
your bodies to God because of all he has done for you.
Let them be a living and holy sacrifice—the kind he will find
acceptable. This is truly the way to worship him. Don't copy
the behavior and customs of this world, but let God
transform you into a new person by changing the way
you think. Then you will learn to know God's will for you,
which is good and pleasing and perfect.*

ROMANS 12:1-2 NLT

Many girls don't understand that their bodies are gifts
from God to be used for His glory. To tell the truth, most
girls see their bodies as a way to attract attention. Yet God
wants you to go against the norm. Several other transla-
tions of the Bible say "don't conform," which means simply
don't copy what everyone else is doing. As followers of
Jesus, God wants you to do what you know in your heart is
right. No matter what anyone else does. Be true to God and
follow His leading in your heart.

*Dear God, a lot of the girls I know are using their bodies
in a way that doesn't please You. Help me not to
get caught up in that. Please transform
my thoughts to match Your thoughts.*

Pleasing God

*Finally, dear brothers and sisters, we urge you in the name
of the Lord Jesus to live in a way that pleases God,
as we have taught you. You live this way already,
and we encourage you to do so even more.*

1 THESSALONIANS 4:1 NLT

When you live your life in a way that pleases God, your life
will look different from people who don't know Him. That's
how it's supposed to be. Jesus said in John 15:19 (NIV), "If
you belonged to the world, it would love you as its own. As
it is, you do not belong to the world, but I have chosen you
out of the world." This doesn't mean you have to follow a
bunch of rules about how you can look and how you can't.
God is not asking you to be weird or to turn your nose up
at other people. He's asking you to just come to Him and
get His approval on the things you do and say, the clothes
you wear, and the attitude of your heart. Pleasing God
isn't as hard as people think. . .God just wants you to talk to
Him about everything and listen to what He says in return.

*God, I really want to please You. I want to know Your
plans and purpose for me. Take hold of my heart,
Lord. It's all Yours!*

Filled with Purity and Love

*The purpose of my instruction is that all believers would be
filled with love that comes from a pure heart,
a clear conscience, and genuine faith.*

1 TIMOTHY 1:5 NLT

Timothy was a young church leader that Paul was mentoring. Paul wrote the book of 1 Timothy as a letter of encouragement and teaching for Timothy. Paul's main goal as a missionary is stated here in verse 5: he teaches so that all believers will be filled with love from a pure heart, clear conscience, and real-life faith. When you read certain parts of the Bible without looking at the whole context, you might get a little confused about some of the rules. Jesus himself tells us that loving God and loving others is really all that matters. Paul repeats that message again and again. The Christian life is all about love from a pure heart. When it becomes more about rules and religion. . .that is not genuine faith in Christ. God's hope for you as a young person is that you'll be filled with purity and love. Ask Him to guard your heart.

*God, thank You that Your purpose for me is love
and purity. Please guard my heart as I grow up.
Fill me with Your love and presence.*

Clean Spoons

*If you keep yourself pure, you will be a special utensil for
honorable use. Your life will be clean, and you will be ready
for the Master to use you for every good work.*

2 TIMOTHY 2:21 NLT

If you're getting ready to eat your morning cereal, you pull
a spoon out of the silverware drawer and you expect it to
be clean, right? It's ready for you to use it to fill your body
with breakfast. This verse in 2 Timothy is kinda the same
thing. If you're clean before God, you're ready for Him to
use you! If you live your life to honor God and talk to Him
about the good and not-so-good in your heart every day. . .
God will use you. He wants to use all of us to do great
things, but only those who live clean lives are ready for
whatever God wants to do with their lives. If you found a
dirty spoon in the silverware drawer, would you still use
it to eat your cereal? Ew. . .gross! Nope, you'd put it in the
dishwasher and go look for a clean spoon, right? Keep that
in mind if you want to be used by God!

*God, please give me a clean heart.
Help me to live a clean life so that You can use me.*

Pure Wisdom

*But the wisdom from above is first of all pure. It is also
peace loving, gentle at all times, and willing to yield to
others. It is full of mercy and the fruit of good deeds.
It shows no favoritism and is always sincere.*

JAMES 3:17 NLT

Lots of people head straight to the internet whenever they
need wisdom. They google everything, looking for answers
to all of their questions. The answers they find, however,
are rarely pure, peace-loving, gentle, and unselfish. You
might find the answer you're looking for, but it will be
mixed with thousands of differing opinions and you have
to sift through a bunch of junk to find some truth. Pure wisdom is rarely found online unless you're looking up God's
Word! When you need wisdom, the Bible tells us that we
can ask God for it and He'll give it to us! Just because we
asked Him (see James 1:5)! You never have to sift through
any questionable content to find wisdom from God. He will
give you pure answers that promote peace and love.

*God, I definitely need lots of wisdom in this mixed-up world.
Sometimes I get very confused about what is right and
wrong. Please give me the desire to come to You for the
answers to all my questions.*

Your Inheritance

All praise to God, the Father of our Lord Jesus Christ. It is by his great mercy that we have been born again, because God raised Jesus Christ from the dead. Now we live with great expectation, and we have a priceless inheritance— an inheritance that is kept in heaven for you, pure and undefiled, beyond the reach of change and decay.

1 PETER 1:3-4 NLT

Wealthy families leave an inheritance for their children. All of their earthly possessions get passed to someone else when they die because. . .as you probably know. . .you can't take anything with you! Kings and queens passed their fortunes and crowns down to their children, and God does that same for you! If you have trusted Christ as your Savior. . .you have been born again as a daughter of the High King! You're His princess, and He keeps your inheritance safe in heaven for all eternity. Now you can live the rest of your life with great expectation. . .knowing what awaits you in heaven!

God, I love that You're my father—and that makes me a daughter of the King! I will follow You all the days of my life expecting that all Your dreams for me will come true.

Pure and Blameless

And so, dear friends, while you are waiting for these things
to happen, make every effort to be found living peaceful
lives that are pure and blameless in his sight.

2 PETER 3:14 NLT

Being pure and blameless sounds like such an impossible task, doesn't it? That's because it is. There is absolutely no way that you can keep yourself pure and blameless in your own strength. If you could, you wouldn't need Jesus, right? God tells us that what is impossible with us, is possible with Him (see Luke 18:27)! The only way that you can live a pure and blameless life in this confusing world is in the power of Jesus Christ Himself. Ask Him to invade your life and to be real to you in every way. The Spirit of God is living in You and gives you the same power that raised Jesus from the grave! It is only through Jesus, though. When you think you can do it on your own. . .that's when everything comes crashing down.

God, I know there is no way I can be pure and blameless
on my own. Please come in and take over my life.
Help me to be all that You want me to be so that
I can live a life of joy and love forever.

Keep Pure

*Dear friends, we are already God's children, but he has not
yet shown us what we will be like when Christ appears.
But we do know that we will be like him, for we will see him
as he really is. And all who have this eager expectation
will keep themselves pure, just as he is pure.*

1 JOHN 3:2-3 NLT

. . . .

Soon, we will be able to see Christ as He really is. The
Bible tells us amazing things that will happen to us in
the end times. While we wait, God wants us to be pure,
like He is. Remember, we can't do this on our own. Check
out 2 Corinthians 3:17–18 (NIV) that says, "Now the Lord
is the Spirit, and where the Spirit of the Lord is, there is
freedom. And we all, who with unveiled faces contemplate
the Lord's glory, are being transformed into his image
with ever-increasing glory, which comes from the Lord,
who is the Spirit." If you are a follower of Christ, you are
being transformed into His likeness day by day! His Spirit
invades your life and changes you. . .keeping you pure for
what is to come.

*God, thank You for Your Spirit that is always at work within
me. Thank You that I don't have to be afraid or worried that
I have to do this all on my own. I'm Yours, Lord!*

Virtue and Self-Control

For this very reason, make every effort to supplement your faith with virtue, and virtue with knowledge, and knowledge with self-control, and self-control with steadfastness, and steadfastness with godliness, and godliness with brotherly affection, and brotherly affection with love.

2 PETER 1:5-7 ESV

We don't hear a lot about virtue and self-control in today's culture. Being a girl of virtue means that you pursue goodness and purity instead of trying to fit in with the crowd. Our enemy, Satan, is out to trip up young people in any way he can. He often aims his arrows right at your purity, telling you that you're not cool if you don't wear what other girls are wearing, trying to get you to believe you're not beautiful unless you have a boyfriend, urging you to look at something you know you shouldn't online, etc. Those are all tricks and lies from the pit of hell. Don't believe them! Instead, ask God to fill you up with His power to overcome all the tricks of the enemy. Check out 1 Corinthians 10:13 and commit that to memory. God always provides a way out of temptation!

God, please help me to look for the escape routes You put in my path every time I'm tempted to do wrong.

Why Be Shy?

*For God gave us a spirit not of fear
but of power and love and self-control.*
2 TIMOTHY 1:7 ESV

. . . .

God has given each of us different personalities, and there is nothing wrong with the way that God hard-wired you! He made some of us outgoing and free-spirited. He made some of us to be curious and to love studying! He made others to be creative and deep thinkers. He made others to be organized and neat. However He made you, He wants you to use that personality to honor Him. While some of us might not like getting up in front of large groups of people, we never, ever have to be afraid of what other people might say or think about us. Only God's opinion of you really matters. He has given you His Spirit who lives inside of you. That is a Spirit of power, love, and self-control. If you are ever feeling extra shy about anything, remember whose Spirit you can depend on. Ask Him to show up in big ways. He always does!

*God, thank You for my personality. You designed me to
think and act a special way. Help me to honor You
with my thoughts and actions.*

You Are a Temple

Do you not know that your bodies are temples of the Holy Spirit, who is in you, whom you have received from God? You are not your own; you were bought at a price. Therefore honor God with your bodies.

1 CORINTHIANS 6:19–20 NIV

When you commit your life to Christ, His Spirit miraculously comes to live inside of you and you become a temple of the Holy Spirit. A Bible dictionary actually defines a temple like this: "any place or object in which God dwells, as the body of a Christian" (see 1 Corinthians 6:19). Isn't that amazing? So if your very own body is a place where God Himself dwells, doesn't that make you want to take care of it a little bit better? We can take care of our temples by eating right, exercising, getting enough rest, dressing modestly, and keeping ourselves pure. Being a temple of the Holy Spirit is a big responsibility, and we can't do it without supernatural help. Ask for God's help to make healthy decisions for your body.

God, help me to take Your words seriously. I believe I am Your temple, and I want to make healthy choices for my body. Please help me to remember this every day.

Everlasting Life

Search me, God, and know my heart; test me and know my anxious thoughts. See if there is any offensive way in me, and lead me in the way everlasting.

PSALM 139:23-24 NIV

. . . .

It doesn't matter how much you know *about* God if you don't know Him personally and believe the truth about what He's done for you. The Bible even says that some who think they know God, really don't (see Matthew 7:21-23)! You either know God personally—you're living for Him and you've allowed Him to change your life—or you don't! Knowing God personally means you're daily choosing God's will over your own. You're pushing down your own selfish desires and asking God what He would have you do—then doing it! Jesus said "I am the way and the truth and the life. No one comes to the Father except through me" (John 14:6). Be sure! You can't know the Father without coming to faith through His Son. If you already know Christ as your Savior, pray for your unsaved friends and family to come to know Him.

God, thank You for saving me and loving me. Give me the courage to share Your message with all those I love.

Love Is the Greatest!

And now these three remain: faith, hope and love.
But the greatest of these is love.
1 CORINTHIANS 13:13 NIV

First Corinthians 13 is known as "the love chapter." If you've ever wondered what love is and what it isn't, check it out: "If I could speak all the languages of earth and of angels, but didn't love others, I would only be a noisy gong or a clanging cymbal. If I had the gift of prophecy, and if I understood all of God's secret plans and possessed all knowledge, and if I had such faith that I could move mountains, but didn't love others, I would be nothing. If I gave everything I have to the poor and even sacrificed my body, I could boast about it; but if I didn't love others, I would have gained nothing (verses 1–3). The chapter goes on to tell us what love is. Basically, if you are the most amazing person in the world, the best preacher, teacher, poet, etc. . . . it means absolutely nothing if you don't have love. Love trumps everything else!

God, please show me what real love is. . .and what it isn't.
I get confused sometimes, but You are the author of love,
and I know You personally! Teach me how to love like You!

A New Heart

*And I will give you a new heart, and I will put a new spirit
in you. I will take out your stony, stubborn heart
and give you a tender, responsive heart.*
EZEKIEL 36:26 NLT

We've been talking about how God gives us His Spirit
when we choose to commit our lives to Christ. God sets
a brand-new heart in each of us. Romans 8:9 (NLT) says,
"But you are not controlled by your sinful nature. You are
controlled by the Spirit if you have the Spirit of God living
in you." (Remember that those who do not have the Spirit
of Christ living in them do not belong to him at all.) God
removes our old stubborn and sinful heart and gives us a
soft and tender heart that yields to Him. Do you wish He
would do that for some of your friends and family, too?
Pray for them every single day. Ask God to soften their
stony heart and give them a new one. Pray for God's love to
shine through you so that they will want what you have.

*God, I pray for my friends and family who aren't fully Yours,
yet. Please give them a new heart and help them
desire to live for You.*

A Clean Heart

Create in me a clean heart, O God,
and renew a right spirit within me.
PSALM 51:10 ESV

King David messed up big time, and yet He was still called a "man after God's own heart." Are you a girl after God's own heart? Do you seek Him and trust Him? Do you run after Him and desire His Presence in Your life? You don't have to be perfect to have a personal relationship with God. Psalm 51 was written by David after he had sinned deeply against God. The prophet Nathan had to go to David to get him to see what he was doing wrong. After David realized his sin, he wrote Psalm 51. Open your Bible and read the entire thing. Have you ever felt this way? Like you've messed up really bad and you need a clean heart? Pray Psalm 51 to God and ask Him to clean out your heart. Through Jesus, God wipes our sin clean and makes our hearts whiter than snow (see verse 7).

God, like David, I've messed up. I still want to be a girl after
Your own heart, Lord. Please forgive my sin and give me
a clean heart. Thank You for Jesus and that
through Him, I am right with You.

Don't Let the Enemy Trip You Up!

It happens so regularly that it's predictable. The moment I decide to do good, sin is there to trip me up. I truly delight in God's commands, but it's pretty obvious that not all of me joins in that delight. Parts of me covertly rebel, and just when I least expect it, they take charge.

ROMANS 7:21-23 MSG

We all make mistakes. Does this scripture ring any bells with you? You've decided that you'll never do something again and then you find yourself doing that same thing again. You get so mad at yourself each time it happens and you feel like you are a complete failure! Don't let the lies of the enemy trip you up! Only Jesus Himself has the right to tell you who you really are. He says He already paid for all of your mistakes. . .past. . .present. . .future. When sin happens again and again. . .take it straight to God. Confess it, and tell Him how you really feel. Ask Him to take control of your life and allow the Spirit of God to change you.

God, I want to do Your will. I'm not getting some things right, and I need Your help. Please fill me with Your Spirit and change my heart.

Loving God

*Let love and faithfulness never leave you; bind them around
your neck, write them on the tablet of your heart.
Then you will win favor and a good name
in the sight of God and man.*

PROVERBS 3:3–4 NIV

To love God you have to know and understand certain
things about Him. John 10:27–30 (NIV) says, "My sheep
listen to my voice; I know them, and they follow me. I give
them eternal life, and they shall never perish; no one will
snatch them out of my hand. My Father, who has given
them to me, is greater than all; no one can snatch them
out of my Father's hand. I and the Father are one." In John
15 Jesus tells us how we can show our love for God: by
obeying His commands. What are His commands? To
love God and love others. Everything else depends on
those two things (see Matthew 22:36–40). In Bible times,
a gentle shepherd would love and care for his sheep with
compassion and kindness. The sheep would listen to the
shepherd's voice. Jesus calls us His sheep and He lovingly
cares for each of us!

*God, please help me to learn how listen to Your voice.
Please help me to be faithful to You always.*

Does God Like Me?

"The LORD your God is with you, the Mighty Warrior who saves. He will take great delight in you; in his love he will no longer rebuke you, but will rejoice over you with singing."

ZEPHANIAH 3:17 NIV

You have probably heard a lot about how much God loves you in your lifetime. However, love and like are a little different, right? Do you think God likes you? Pastor and author Dr. Charles Stanley says this: "Yes, God likes me. He approves of me. He likes spending time with me. He likes being with me. He likes hearing me when I pray to Him, and He also enjoys talking with me through His Word. I believe He loves me. He knows I make mistakes, but He sees my heart and my desire to know Him better each day." When you come to know Jesus as your Savior, God washes all your sins away and He sees you as the perfect girl you are. And you can say with confidence, "God likes me!" He rejoices over you, and the Bible says He even sings about you! You are liked. You are loved. You are His!

Dear God, wow! This makes my heart smile. Thank You for loving me. . .and for liking me just the way I am. Thank You for Jesus and seeing me as perfect. I love You. I like You a whole lot, too.

Value Others

*Do nothing out of selfish ambition or vain conceit. Rather,
in humility value others above yourselves, not looking to your
own interests but each of you to the interests of the others.*
PHILIPPIANS 2:3–4 NIV

A common phrase today is to "look out for number one,
because nobody else will." It's on social media, on bumper
stickers, on T-shirts—but it is completely opposite of what
God wants for us to do. God wants us to put others ahead
of ourselves, to look out for the needs of those around us
and not worry about getting our needs met all the time.
God isn't asking us to be in relationship with people who
will hurt us emotionally or abuse us and allow them to do
whatever they want. No, Jesus Christ set us free, and He
doesn't want anyone else to steal our freedom! He gives us
the freedom to love others and to value them. We are free
people! Free to love and to give of ourselves in the way we
choose. When we choose to love God and His people, He
will make sure that all of our needs are taken care of.

*God, forgive me for the times I've been selfish.
Help me to put others before myself.*

The Desires of Your Heart

Delight yourself in the Lord,
and he will give you the desires of your heart.
PSALM 37:4 ESV

. . . .

Have you ever taken the time to write out all of your wants and needs? Ask God to join you as you write out this list. Start with your basic needs: food, shelter, water, etc. Then move on to the things you really want, like special games or toys. . .and then write what you want to do with your life and the things you want or need to get you there. Make sure you put a date at the top of your list. After you've created your list, hold it before God and ask Him to lead you. Thank Him for the needs that He has already provided. Ask Him for the other items on your list that you need. Then talk to Him about your wants. Do they align with God's will for you? Are they good and God-honoring wants? Do you feel like you don't have enough patience to wait for the things you need and want? Ask God to give you wisdom and patience. Trust Him with your list.

God, I give You all my wants and needs. Help me to delight
myself in You alone, not in the things I think I might want.
I know You will bless me in the way that You think is best.

God's Thoughts

*For my thoughts are not your thoughts, neither are your
ways my ways, declares the LORD. For as the heavens are
higher than the earth, so are my ways higher than
your ways and my thoughts than your thoughts.*

ISAIAH 55:8–9 ESV

Sometimes, well-meaning people put words into God's
mouth. They speak for Him and about Him. . .but sometimes they get it wrong. That's why it's so important to
find out what God says for yourself! The Bible tells us that
God's ways are not our ways. We can only think with our
human minds. . .but God is the one who *made* them! We
can't possibly know all His ways or understand all His
plans. If someone tells you something about God and
you're not sure if it is true or not, the best thing to do is to
go talk to God yourself. Get into His Word and get to know
Him. One of the best books of the Bible to start knowing
God is the book of John. Try reading it this month. Ask
God to come along side you as you read it and give you
wisdom.

*God, I'm so amazed that You want me to have a personal
relationship with You! I can't thank You enough for allowing
me to come straight to You with all of my questions.
Thank You for guiding me!*

Here's How God Sees You

*So Peter went over the side of the boat and walked on the
water toward Jesus. But when he saw the strong wind and
the waves, he was terrified and began to sink.*

MATTHEW 14:29–30 NLT

. . . .

VeggieTales creator Phil Vischer wrote a rhyming script
called "A Snoodle's Tale" about a small and different
creature struggling with self-image. The snoodle is feeling
unloved, unwanted, and low because of his differences and
because of the way others are treating him. So His creator
shows the snoodle a picture of what he really looks like
and says: "Here's what you look like; Here's how I see you.
Keep this in your pack and you'll find it will free you. From
all of the pictures and all of the lies that others make up
just to cut down your size." When you take your eyes off of
Jesus, just like Peter, your self-image will start to sink. You
will feel less beautiful and unloved. When you keep your
eyes on Christ, you'll begin to see yourself as He sees you:
beautiful and just right!

*God, thank You for creating me just the way I am.
Help me to keep my eyes on You so that I will
see myself as You see me.*

God's Purpose for Me

The LORD will fulfill his purpose for me; your steadfast love,
O LORD, endures forever. Do not forsake
the work of your hands.
PSALM 138:8 ESV

You were put on this earth for a purpose. You didn't happen by accident, and the Bible tells us that God knows the number of your days and the number of hairs on your head. Yes, you were brought into this world by your parents, but it is God who determines your purpose. Philippians 1:6 (NLT) says, "And I am certain that God, who began the good work within you, will continue his work until it is finally finished on the day when Christ Jesus returns." God started a good work in you the day you were born. He has great plans for your life (see Jeremiah 29:11–13) and wants to be with you every step of the way. Seek Him for every decision, big or small. . .He wants to walk with you through them all.

God, thanks for creating me! I'm so glad You know
everything about me and want to help me with all my
decisions. Fill me with Your Holy Spirit, and guide
me closer and closer to Your heart.

A Day in the Life

How do you know what your life will be like tomorrow? Your life is like the morning fog—it's here a little while, then it's gone. What you ought to say is, "If the Lord wants us to, we will live and do this or that."

JAMES 4:14–15 NLT

. . . .

Have you ever thought what it would be like if you knew today would be your last day on earth? Would you ask your parents to hop on a plane with you and visit an exotic location? Would you spend your day with the ones you love? Would you do something you've always dreamed of doing but never have? Would you share Jesus with someone that you've never had the courage to talk to before? Life on this planet is pretty short. We never know how long we have to live here. That shouldn't be something that scares us. . .it's just a fact of life. So each day, we really ought to live life like it's our last day on earth. The Bible tells us that Jesus could come back at any moment, too (see Matthew 25:13)!

God, thanks for each minute You've given me on this earth. Help me make the most of each day I'm given.

God's Word Is Truth

*It is the same with my word. I send it out, and it always
produces fruit. It will accomplish all I want it to,
and it will prosper everywhere I send it.*

ISAIAH 55:11 NLT

. . . .

The Bible that you have in your home is an amazing tool
from God. Inside it holds wonders, mysteries, miracles,
adventures. . .and it's all true! Here is the most amazing
thing: it is *alive*! Did you know that? God's Word is alive.
The Bible tells us in Hebrews 4:12 that God's Word is living
and active! Do you know of any other book like that ever
written? The Bible is God-breathed (see 2 Timothy 3:16)
and still very much alive and producing fruit today. God's
Word is how we get to know the truth about who God is
and what He's done. The Holy Spirit uses words from the
Bible to teach us God's will. When you hide God's Word in
your heart, you learn how to live a full and God-honoring
life.

*Wow, God. It's amazing that You sent us a book that is
alive and powerful. We worship You, not the book,
but thank You for loving us so much You gave us an
instruction manual to help us through life. Help me
not to take Your Word for granted.*

Treasured Daughter

"The LORD your God is with you, the Mighty Warrior who saves. He will take great delight in you, in his love he will no longer rebuke you, but will rejoice over you with singing."
ZEPHANIAH 3:17 NIV

What an amazing verse to remind us of who God is and who we are in Him! He delights in us, and He rejoices over us. He is our Father, and we are His treasured daughters. Do you feel like a treasured daughter of the king? If not, what is keeping you from a close communion with your heavenly Father? We are all made perfect in Christ, and we can approach God's throne with confidence (see Hebrews 4:16) because of what Jesus Christ did for us on the cross. Your heavenly Father loves you and wants to have a close father-daughter relationship with you. There is nothing than you can do to earn His love. It is already there for you. There is nothing you can do to make Him love you any more than He already does. His love is everlasting. You are treasured!

God, thank You for being with me. Help me to know and feel that I am deeply loved by You. In Jesus' name, amen.

The Only Thing That Counts

*The only thing that counts is faith
expressing itself through love.*
GALATIANS 5:6 NIV

Mother Teresa said: "Let us always meet each other with smile, for the smile is the beginning of love." Can you try that today? Even if you really don't feel like smiling, remember to be the light in someone else's dark world. Ask God to fill you with His love today so that you can share that with everyone you meet. The Bible promises that when we are weak, God is strong (see 2 Corinthians 12:9–10). So if you're feeling low and you don't have a smile left to share, remember that God can be your strength for you. He can help you love like Jesus loved. That is the only thing that really counts.

*God, sometimes I get so caught up in my feelings
and the stress of life that I forget what really matters:
Your love! That's it! That's what You put me here for—
to love You and to love others. Be my strength today,
and help me love people through You.*

It Is Good to Be Near God

But as for me, it is good to be near God. I have made the
Sovereign Lord my refuge; I will tell of all your deeds.
PSALM 73:28 NIV

Years ago, a youth pastor told his audience to "get so close to God that you smell like Him!" How is that even possible? How can an invisible God be close to us? There is a true story of a premature baby that defied the odds. The parents were told that the baby would not live, and they were not even able to touch her for two months as she was hooked to machines. Yet God answered the prayers of this family, and she grew into a healthy little girl. At the age of five, the little girl told her mom she smelled God outside. Her mom, knowing that it was an approaching thunderstorm, told her it was just the smell of rain. Yet the little girl was adamant that it was the smell of God. She told her mom that it smelled like God when you lay your head on His chest.

God, I can't see the wind, but I know it's there...
just like You. Remind me that You're always near.
Thank You for loving me!

Scripture Index